The Liberating Word

The
Liberating
Word

A GUIDE
TO NONSEXIST INTERPRETATION
OF THE BIBLE

Edited by Letty M. Russell

*In cooperation with the
Task Force on Sexism in the Bible
Division of Education and Ministry
National Council of the Churches of Christ
in the U.S.A.*

THE WESTMINSTER PRESS
Philadelphia

Scripture quotations from the Revised Standard Version of the Bible are copyright, 1946 and 1952, by the Division of Christian Education of the National Council of Churches, and are used by permission.

Book Design by Dorothy Alden Smith

Published by The Westminster Press ®
Philadelphia, Pennsylvania

PRINTED IN THE UNITED STATES OF AMERICA

Library of Congress Cataloging in Publication Data

Main entry under title:

The Liberating word.

Bibliography: p.
1. Sex (Theology)—Biblical teaching—Addresses, essays, lectures. 2. Woman (Theology)—Biblical teaching—Addresses, essays, lectures. 3. Bible—Criticism, interpretation, etc.—Addresses, essays, lectures. I. Russell, Letty M. II. National Council of the Churches of Christ in the United States of America. Task Force on Sexism in the Bible.
BS680.S5L5   220.6   76–18689
ISBN 0–664–24751–2

CONTENTS

FOREWORD

Emily V. Gibbes
Valerie Russell

One of the goals of the Division of Education and Ministry of the National Council of Churches is to provide leadership and resources that support and facilitate the church as a Biblically informed community of faith and action. Along with other agencies and institutions specifically concerned with making the Biblical witness available and understood, the Division helps to provide leadership and resources for the churches' commitment to be and to become a Biblically rooted community of faith and action.

An effort to implement that goal, probably more than anything else, is at the heart of our presenting this Guide to a large segment of the Bible-reading and Bible-studying community. THE LIBERATING WORD: A GUIDE TO NONSEXIST INTERPRETATION OF THE BIBLE is the Division of Education and Ministry's effort to draw pastors and lay people into finding ways for making worship and study more inclusive of all participants.

Members of the Division of Education and Ministry have been made conscious by the stirrings about sexist assumptions in the church and in the world at large. We have been stimulated by the questions that men and

9

women are asking as they recognize the true liberating force of the Scriptures and of theology, We have been alerted by the insistence of task forces on women within our various churches—especially those concerned with liturgical language and language about God—that language is important in addressing problems of discrimination.

Our consciousness has come alive in recent years to the sexist language and sex stereotypes in the literature that we read and other resources that we hear and see. Publishers have developed guidelines for the treatment of the sexes in all their publications, and thus have alerted their authors and staff members to the problems of sex discrimination and to various ways of solving them. The University of the State of New York has developed guidelines for "Reviewing Curriculum for Sexism" in all the schools and institutions in the state. There have been studies of several denominational Christian education curricula to discover sex stereotypes and sexist language. These are only a few of the evidences of concern that have recently come to our attention. At a time when we are discovering clearly the reciprocal nature of language, social structure, and social behavior, we are forced to examine everything from literature to history for its reference, or lack of reference, to women. We are also forced to face the question, What of the Bible? How do we help those who study, teach, and interpret the Bible now to deal with sexism in the Bible? How do we act in the light of our purpose to provide leadership and resources to help enable the church to become a Biblically rooted community?

Seeking thus to be responsive to its goal and to what is happening in church and society, a Task Force on

Sexism in the Bible was established with a mandate to develop recommendations to the Division of Education and Ministry on problems of context and ways to use Biblical material which compensate for its sexism. Now, after two years of work by the task force, the Division presents this book—a guide for the practitioner—for women, men, youth, pastors and laity in churches, study groups, college students and seminarians who read, study, and interpret the Bible today. THE LIBERATING WORD is a guide for the people who are willing to work on nonsexist interpretation of the Bible now. It is a beginning step as we encourage a new generation of female and male Bible scholars to develop new Bibles and commentaries.

The task of understanding the roots of Bible language and of developing new language consistent with our heritage and the contemporary situation is tremendous. We trust that THE LIBERATING WORD: A GUIDE TO NONSEXIST INTERPRETATION OF THE BIBLE will truly be for you a liberating word. The Division of Education and Ministry offers the work of these four Christian women as an opportunity to begin the conversation with men and women who are struggling today with questions of inclusive language in worship and discussion. Additional resources for your further study are also included.

We wish to thank a number of people for their support of and contribution to the effort involved in writing this book. To all the members of the Task Force on Sexism in the Bible and to the Division of Education and Ministry with its creative and emancipated thinking we owe the reality of this book. To the authors— Sharon H. Ringe, Elisabeth Schüssler Fiorenza, Joanna Dewey—who in spite of heavy teaching schedules and the difficulty of research in their field of scholarship, were willing to join in the dialogue, writing during their vacation periods. And finally, no words are adequate to express our appreciation to Letty M. Russell, author-editor and theologian, whose clear insight, commitment, experience, and hard work put the book into final form and who added resources and questions to enable it to be used as a study guide.

INTRODUCTION:
THE LIBERATING WORD

Letty M. Russell

This Guide to nonsexist interpretation of the Bible is both long overdue and premature. It is long overdue because almost one hundred years have passed since Christian women in the United States began to make collective attempts to overcome ways in which the Bible is used as a means of reinforcing their subordination to men through divine sanction. In 1895, Elizabeth Cady Stanton and a committee of women published an interpretation of the passages "directly referring to women, and those also in which women are made prominent by exclusion."[1] These and many other efforts have had little impact on the perspectives of Bible scholars or members of local churches. This Guide is an overdue attempt to draw laypeople and pastors of many churches into dialogue and investigation of the possibilities for making worship and study more inclusive of all participants, both women and men.

The Guide is premature because everything here suggested is experimental in nature. At the moment, we do not have any consensus on how to reflect the changing consciousness of women and men about their roles as human beings in regard to the ways we translate and interpret Scripture. There are, however, many women and men who are struggling daily with questions of inclusive language in worship and discussion. All of us need to assist one another to find our way, not only through more inclusive forms of liturgy, hymns, and theology but also through more inclusive ways of interpreting Scripture.[2] We cannot wait for a new generation of female and male scholars to publish new Bible translations and commentaries that eliminate the hitherto unconscious sexist bias of writers, most of whom are male. Right now, women sit with men in the pews of the churches. Right now, women and men study theology and learn to preach and teach. Right now, children are being taught, directly and indirectly, the message of the Bible. Thus, this "premature" book is issued, not as a finished product, but as an invitation to readers to join in the discussion and interpretation in new and creative ways.

I. *The Liberating Word and Liberating the Word*

The Word of God is living and liberating to those who hear with faith and live it out in faith. The Biblical message becomes good news to each successive generation as the power of the Holy Spirit conveys this message through the study and action of Christian communities. Because the gospel speaks in ever-new ways to changing situations, we have nothing to fear from listening to it afresh as our consciousness and experience change.

The universal message of God's love for all humankind will continue to be heard through the power of the Holy Spirit, but the fashion in which it is heard depends on our willingness to speak and act the Word in ways

concretely addressed to the struggles and longings of
women and men today. Today, that speaking and acting
can no longer ignore the existence of women as part of
the people of God. Women are no longer willing to be
invisible partners either in the work and life of church
and society or in the interpretation and proclamation of
the gospel. The Word must be concretely addressed to
their journey toward freedom as well as to that of others.

In a sense, this "premature" Guide is very preten-
tious. It dares to invite Christians everywhere to join in
a risky task: that of liberating the Word from sexist
interpretations that continue to dominate our thoughts
and actions. The Word of God is liberating and the
power of the Holy Spirit continues to enliven it among
us. But how about the words of men? The Bible was
written in a patriarchal culture in which the father was
supreme in clan, family, and nation, and wives and children were legally dependent.[3] The interpretation and
translation of the Bible through the centuries has been
carried out in societies and Christian communities that
are male-centered, or androcentric.[4] Just as non-West-
ern cultures must seek to liberate the white, Western
interpretations of Scripture and theology so that they
are heard anew in different cultures and subcultures,
women must seek to liberate the interpretation of
God's Word from male bias.

This is a task initiated by women of deep Christian
conviction, women who believe that sexism is a sin because it declares one half of the human race inferior
because of their biology. The Bible tells us that both
male and female are made in God's image (Gen. 1:27).
It tells us that Jesus Christ died for us all (Mark 10:45).
As both women and men begin to discover the possibil-

ity of new forms of wholeness and partnership, they
must also work together to liberate the Word to be
God's Word of freedom and new life, addressed to all
people in all situations of life.

II. *Language and Liberation*

In seeking to heed the call of Christ to freedom and
unity, the way we use language is an indicator of our
commitment to the full human community. In every
culture, language plays an important role in addressing
problems of discrimination in church and society. We
cannot be true to the gospel message if we preach it in
ways that often ignore large portions of the human race.
Our words reflect the nature of reality as we see it, and
they can be a powerful tool, either for oppression or
liberation.

Language and social structures are reciprocal in relationship. Language not only shapes given concepts of
reality and ways of acting, it is also shaped by changes
in concepts and social behavior. Generally, the ruling
group of a given society tends to impose its value system
through the connotations of language usage. Powerless
groups usually have little part in the formation of standard language and tend to internalize the social structures mirrored in that language.

Therefore, if a powerless group becomes conscious of
its subordinate relationship to the ruling group and is in
the process of self-liberation, it is necessary for newly
created relationships to find expression in new language and imagery. Without a conscious change in ex-
pressions, the desired process of change in oppressive
social structures is slowed down.

The type of Biblical and theological language used in

church services of worship, discussion groups, educational institutions, and publications still tends to exclude women from the Christian community. More and more, women are becoming conscious of their social exclusion reflected in that language and are resisting these subtle and not so subtle forms of discrimination. They are uneasy about phrases like "God the Father loves you." "If you join the brotherhood and fellowship of all Christians, you will become sons of God!" As long as the language of Christian churches creates the feeling that one group is inferior and another group is superior, it ruptures the unity in Jesus Christ, who is the center of the Christian community.[5]

In translating and interpreting Scripture, we are making not only social but also theological affirmations about God and ourselves as partners with Christ in God's new creation struggling to be born. We confess our faith in the God of the Hebrew people, the God of Jesus Christ who is known through the history of the church and of all humanity. This God transcends all categories of male and female. The pronouns and images we use point to the mystery of God, who is both *beyond* our human comprehension and yet *with us.* In order to relate to God personally in worship and faith, we may ascribe to God both feminine and masculine cultural metaphors as descriptions of our own changing human experience. When we use both feminine and masculine metaphors for God, we are not trying to reinforce stereotyped sex roles of a particular culture. Instead, we are trying to reflect a spectrum of those metaphors, so that our images of ourselves and of God can be expanded and become more whole.

We can do this because we are *theomorphic,* made in God's image.[6] As human beings, we are able to relate to

God in trust and love, using a wide range of human experience to express this faith. Our experience is drawn not only from two thousand years of Biblical history but also from nearly two thousand years of post-Biblical history. The story of the Bible relates to us as a history of God with persons. In this sense, God is seen as a *humanist.* God has been clearly revealed in Jesus Christ as One who cares for and desires to be with human beings.[7] And if God is a humanist, then surely, using contemporary language, God is a *feminist:* One who "shows no partiality" (Acts 10:34) but calls and accepts people regardless of their sex.[8]

Some people may suggest that the use of more inclusive language in translation and interpretation will present a stumbling block to the faith of those who are comfortable with traditional language. Certainly we must take Paul's words seriously: "Only take care lest this liberty of yours somehow become a stumbling block to the weak" (I Cor. 8:9).[9] Changes must be made carefully and with regard for those who find them difficult. Yet we must balance the problems of change with the dangers of stumbling that the traditional liberty of a male-dominated culture presents for many women today. Our practices in traditional language run at least three risks. First, they reinforce inferiority and superiority stereotypes. Second, they are causing the alienation of some women from the life and worship of the church because the consciousness of these women no longer allows them to accept exclusive language. Third, they run the risk of making God too small! If we think of God as a baal or idol of one group, we are forgetting the mystery of One who cares for all human beings and welcomes their love.

III. *Taking the Bible Seriously*

Perhaps many people who see this Guide to nonsexist interpretation of the Bible will say, "Why bother?" They might argue that the Bible was written long ago in different cultural settings and it so much reflects the androcentric culture and religion of its time that the message continues to be one of the subordination of women to men, whatever you do with it. To this we can say only that "the liberating Word" has managed to speak in many new languages and cultures. It speaks to people who never saw a desert, let alone a sheepfold or a king. Its message of God's love and justice transcends all cultural barriers when it is lived out in Christian communities of faith. "The liberating Word" can also speak to women and men of today if our words and actions put the gospel into practice as good news of liberty for "those who are oppressed" (Luke 4:18).

From a Christian point of view, the Biblical story is a communal witness to this Word made flesh in a certain time and place in history. It invites us to join that story with God as followers of Jesus Christ. Christian women are part of that history, and they have no intention of being "included out." They take the Bible seriously because, through God's Spirit, it also speaks to them as a liberating Word. Therefore, they want to bother! They want to join with their brothers in translation, research, and interpretation, so that the Word can be heard in changing social and cultural patterns.

This Guide is an invitation to all women and men to work together toward a more holistic and inclusive interpretation of the Biblical message for our time. By means of explanation, interpretation, and suggestions

for translation, it seeks to provide assistance to those
who want to take the Bible seriously and are concerned
with issues of nonsexist interpretation.[10] Those who
share the view of the writers that the Bible is an important source of our own faith will want to join in this task
in their own local situations. As they experiment with
new ideas and images, many more problems and clues
than this book could ever mention can be found and
shared.

Some may be particularly concerned with the problems of translation. As they seek out more accurate
contemporary words and phrases and struggle with
pronoun usage, they should remember that every translation from Hebrew and Greek is itself an interpretation. Translation is the way we continually try to express the original meaning as accurately as possible, so
that it will be understood in different and changing
language and culture. For this reason the work of translation is never completed. To aid those who wish to join
in this task, Sharon H. Ringe, in Chapter 1, "Biblical
Authority and Interpretation," has given suggestions
about the nature of the Biblical texts and their authority, transmission, and interpretation.

Others may want to focus on interpretation of the
meaning of Biblical accounts, so that they come alive to
the ears of women and men today. They will perhaps
discover new stories and metaphors for use in preaching and teaching, those which move beyond the text to
address people's fears, longings, and experience today.
Chapter 2, "Interpreting Patriarchal Traditions," can
be a starting point for groups that want to know more
about the old traditions as they search for new metaphors. Elisabeth Schüssler Fiorenza provides examples
of androcentric (male-centered) traditions and some

ways of dealing with them.

Still others may be more interested in research into and exegesis of the meaning of the Biblical accounts. Many new insights will be discovered as we look at stories from the perspective of women as well as men. This may often lead to new ways of telling Biblical stories and searching out images of women that transcend patriarchal traditions. Joanna Dewey, in Chapter 3, "Images of Women," has provided illustrations of the difference this perspective may make.

Because this Guide is for study and action in local churches and church-related groups, many questions will arise about the theological and practical aspects of developing inclusive language. There are no easy answers, and each group will have to work out its own alternatives in each situation. In Chapter 4, "Changing Language and the Church," Letty Russell explores some suggestions for those who are willing to risk the use of this Guide as a beginning point for change. The sections Additional Resources and Suggestions for Study and Action are provided for individuals and groups engaged in searching out their own forms of interpretation.

Wherever we start with our study, we can all be encouraged by the fact that it is not only this Guide which is both long overdue and premature. The gospel itself and our lives as we live out its message share the same ambiguities. As Paul points out, "The whole creation has been groaning in travail together until now" (Rom. 8:21–22). Even we ourselves are different only in that we groan more deeply because we have already caught a glimpse of that "glorious liberty" which is long overdue. At the same time, the good news of the inbreaking new age of freedom is also premature. It pushes us to live in the present as heirs of that liberty which has already arrived in Jesus Christ (I Cor. 7:29–31). This means that we are constantly restless to get an ever-new glimpse of the liberating Word of God as it teaches us to dream dreams and live out visions of the new creation and community in the present. Perhaps in some small way this Guide may help us as we live out our dreams and visions, ever continuing the story of Acts, ch. 2, as God's Spirit is poured out upon us, so that "sons and daughters shall prophesy" and "whoever calls on the name of the Lord shall be saved" (vs. 17–21).

1
BIBLICAL AUTHORITY
AND INTERPRETATION

Sharon H. Ringe

"The Bible is the Word of God." Christians have always said this. They have believed it, too, but over the years and among the various members of the Christian community it has meant different things. For some, to call the Bible the "Word of God" means that God dictated it verbatim to Moses on Mt. Sinai, and in later times through the agency of the Holy Spirit to prophets, evangelists, and apostles. Others speak of a general "inspiration" of these writers: God inspired or infused their lives with the Holy Spirit, but the actual words chosen are their own. For still others who are aware of internal disagreements in the accounts (the two creation stories in Genesis, for example, or the differences in wording and chronology of the Gospels), God's authority is seen in the accepted interpretation of the stories developed and held through the years by the church.

However it may be meant, to call the Bible the Word of God is an awesome assertion. People have used that assertion and the Bible itself as a means of stifling opposition, enforcing set opinions and understandings, defining the church membership, stalling change, and defending abuse. Yet we who are writing this book also call the Bible the Word of God—God's "liberating Word." We affirm the importance of returning to it, rereading it, and recovering its power for our own lives. And so, before we go on to talk specifically about how women and men are learning to read the familiar and unfamiliar stories of the Bible, it is important to set out our understanding of the Bible: what kind of book it is, how it came into being, what the nature of its authority is, and, as a beginning point, what we mean when *we* call it the Word of God.

I. *The Word of God*

To say that the Bible is the Word of God means indeed that it is a *word from God.* This is a way of affirming, above all, that the initiative in the God-human relationship has been God's. In the Judeo-Christian understanding, this is a covenant relationship. This covenant, or mutually binding agreement, is not one of mechanical reciprocity, but of God's gracious action and our joyful, free response; God's freedom and ours to be with and for each other. The human part of the obligation is embodied in such places as the Ten Commandments, the Golden Rule, the Great Commandment (Mark 12:29–31), or in the prophetic words, "And what does the Lord require of you but to do justice, and to love kindness, and to walk humbly with your God?" (Micah 6:8). All these words from God are set in the context of a recitation of God's words and deeds on behalf of humankind. The other side to the word from God in the form of commandments is the active word/deed (the Hebrew word *dābār* is used for both word and deed) about the obligations, commitments, and in-ments God has taken on. The declarative word about who God is and how God has been known in history precedes the imperative word from God concerning the style of human response.

Thus the Bible is also the *word about God.* People in some religious traditions have statues, models, or propositional statements by which they can capture the divine essence and hold their gods to themselves, but the God whose story is told in the Bible is not like that. God's name YHWH[11] is a verb form: "I am who I am," or "I will be who I will be." As the book of Revelation says, YHWH is "the one who is and who was and who is coming" (Rev. 1:8).[12] YHWH is a God who is known in actions. The word about this God is appropriately a collection of stories about how God has been perceived at work in the midst of and on behalf of the world, which is said to be God's own creation. God is depicted not only as creator but also as the One involved with humankind in the events that comprise world history as that history has been understood by the people of God.

II. *Biblical Authority*

In a real sense, the Bible is a communal work of God's people. Although we call it "Scripture" (*hē graphē,* "that which is written"), writing or even editing by a single hand was a fairly late stage in the development of both the Old and the New Testament stories about God's actions. The stories that we find collected in the Pentateuch, or the first five books of the Bible, for example, probably began as stories told around the campfires of the nomadic Israelites as they wandered across the ancient Near East toward the land which they understood to be their promised home. In the New Testa-

ment, the Gospels also probably began as remembered
anecdotes and teachings of Jesus shared among groups
of disciples as they gathered to sort out what had happened to them and to the One they had followed in the
days leading up to Good Friday and Easter. Even Paul's
letters, which did have a "literary" beginning, bear witness to and incorporate such traditions and stories (I
Cor. 11:23; 15:3–8).

Today scholars are able to use the skills of historical
and literary criticism to analyze Biblical books and to
recover not only the meaning of the texts as we have
them in the Bible but also some of the layers of their
composition, both written and oral. Different records of
the same event (often intricately interwoven), breaks in
the flow of the narrative, changes of pronouns, abrupt
changes of subject or location, and editorial connecting
phrases and sentences are clues to where originally separate stories, or collections of stories, have been brought
together into larger units. Frequently, editorial com-
ments betraying a later historical period or the position,
emphasis, and highlighting of a particular story help us
recognize what a later community found important in
stories about their past. Layers of such compilations can
be discerned in both the Old and the New Testament
as the gathering together of groups of people with a
variety of stories resulted in the blending not only of the
population groups but also of their histories and traditions. These traditions helped them to answer questions
about identity and life-style: Who are we? and, How
should we live? The new subdiscipline of canonical criticism is leading scholars into the pursuit of how the
various traditions and parts of the Bible functioned in
the lives of subsequent generations of the believing

community, and how they eventually came to be understood as authoritative, as containing the essential founding, guiding, and identifying story of that community and people.[13]

For the people who collected and preserved them, the Biblical stories helped describe who they were and how they should live. The identity came in the form of stories of who God is and how God is perceived to be acting in human history, and, thus, who the people are in relationship to God. Questions of life-style came as the people faced the problem of how, then, to live if God is who God seems to be. The fact that these stories spoke to both the major questions of identity and life-style accounts for their being retold and preserved. This is important to keep in mind. It was not because these stories were said to be authoritative that they were told and preserved. Rather, they were told, compiled, and preserved because they spoke to the real needs of the communities out of which they grew and in which they lodged. It was on the power and ability of the stories to speak to basic questions of life that their "authority" rested and still rests, and came eventually to be affirmed and ratified by official pronouncement and the formal process of defining the "canon" or extent of Scripture. The true canonical process is in the keeping and telling of the stories. The stories work, they lend meaning, and they provide a locus for identity and a resource for answering problems of life. Therefore, they are seen as "authoritative," as containing an authentic word from and about God.

Taken as a whole, the Biblical word has many mean-

ings and presents a variety of pictures of the relationship between creator and created order. On the one
hand, we might wonder at the variety. Why does it take
all these stories to present the total picture? On the
other hand, we might ask why only *these* stories have
been included and not others, from a later period or
about other people? For a long time there was considerable disagreement among the churches about which
books did have authority and which ones were, at best,
interesting, or even in fact dangerous. The history of
the debate over the process by which the extent of the
canon became officially set is a long and fascinating one.
The list of New Testament books became fixed very
early, with Hebrews and Revelation being the last seri-
ous points of contention. The extent of the Old Testament canon is still a subject of disagreement in ecumenical discussions, since the Catholic canon includes
several books (Tobit, Ecclesiasticus, Maccabees, and
others) that the Protestant canon lists only in The Apoc-
rypha. However, to repeat, the real canonical process is
not encapsulated in the official decisions of synods and
councils by which books are officially declared in or out
of the canon, nor is the ongoing debate exclusively concerned with whether a specific additional work ought to
be included. The canonical process that led to the formation of the Biblical books and canon continues in the
same way, as people read the stories and rediscover
themselves in them. The premise of a "closed" canon is
not that God ceased to act decisively in human history
after the Bible was written, but rather that in the depth
and variety of these stories, all has been said that is
necessary in order for us to know God's style and priori-
ties and for us to have the *canon* (measuring stick) by
which to judge all subsequent experiences. It is a grow-

ing, lively process with a book of stories that are far from being dead letters.

III. *Biblical Interpretation*

The process of bringing together the ancient canonical texts and new, changing situations is the process of interpretation. The Greek word *hermeneia,* from which the word "hermeneutics" is derived, means: (1) translation, as from one language to another; (2) interpretation, as in the discussion of meaning; (3) expression, saying aloud in words.[14] With that threefold meaning, hermeneutics becomes a useful word by which to talk about what we are doing in this book and what we invite you to do with us.

Interpretation of Biblical stories and traditions is a process that goes back into the Bible itself. Very early in the life of the people of Israel their remembered story included the events of the exodus, God's remarkable deliverance of them from the hands of their Egyptian captors and patient journey with them to the land that had been promised them. This story was a point of pride for the people. By it they knew their chosenness and their special covenant relationship with God. But in a later time when comfort in the land had led to complacency, and economic well-being had led to oppression of the poor in their society, the prophet Amos read the exodus story afresh as grounds for a divine indictment of the people who had misidentified with the story and not seen that they were now in the place of the captors *from whom* deliverance was required:

Hear this word that the Lord has spoken against you, O people of Israel, against the whole family which I brought up out of the land of Egypt:

> "You only have I known
>   of all the families of the earth;
> therefore I will punish you
>   for all your iniquities."
>   (Amos 3:1–2.)

Similarly, at times of crisis in Israel's history, the editors of Deuteronomy and such prophets as Amos, Hosea, and Jeremiah concentrated on the period of Israel's history just before the people entered the Land of Canaan. Deuteronomy ends the story there, although the editors clearly knew of the people's life in the land. The prophets kept referring to God's rescue and deliverance from Egypt, sustenance in the wilderness, and leading to the Promised Land as the record of God's great saving acts toward a more or less faithful people. The time of living in that land, however, they painted as a time of increasing unfaithfulness and disobedience of the people and grief for YHWH. The land, which in brighter times was seen as God's permanent gift to the people of Israel, came to be seen rather as God's trust to the people. In the face of threats and assaults from within and outside the country, these prophets began to reread their own story and realize that when the stewardship of that land and life in the land were violated, when the covenant relationship was broken, the trust could and would be revoked. What then, they began to ask, is Israel without the land, and how can its connections with its God be sustained? The answer would come not in the part of their story that told how Israel lived with kings, Temple, and Holy City as proof of their chosenness, but in how Israel lived without the land, when they knew most vividly God's intercession and bias toward the oppressed and God's prejudice for the homeless and dispossessed.

In the New Testament, Jesus also engaged in the process of interpreting the stories and religious traditions that he received. In the Sermon on the Mount, for example, Jesus encounters head on the question of his relationship to his tradition. "Think not," he said, "that I have come to abolish the law and the prophets; I have come not to abolish them but to fulfil them" (Matt. 5:17). Yet his fulfillment included a radical critique and an enlivening of what had become dead injunctions into once again vital laws for the people, as can be seen in the succession of contrasts ("You have heard that it was said. . . . But I say . . .") concerning anger, lust, divorce, oath-taking, retribution, and love of enemies (Matt. 5:21–48). In each case, the new law was a strengthening and radicalizing of the old. In the case of the law on divorce, Jesus specifically corrected an abuse against women who were subject to divorce without defense or recourse at their husbands' whims. Jesus' concern for women, for the poor, for sinners and outcasts, and for all who fell outside the pale of chosenness and acceptability among the Jews is amply evidenced throughout the Gospels as he reworked standards of etiquette and human behavior into more person-oriented norms.

What was from Jesus essentially a prophetic critique against abuses of the best in Jewish tradition came to be seen as constitutive of the church, substantiating its claim over against that of Judaism to be the true Israel, heir of the promises and the convenant. As the events of the crucifixion and resurrection gave the early church new lenses by which to look at the man Jesus and what he taught and did among them, it also incorporated its new understanding into what had been re-

ceived. The faith and religion *of* Jesus quickly became
faith in or belief *about* Jesus, a religion of which he was
the focal point. Having proclaimed Jesus as the promised Savior and God's Anointed One, the church moved
quickly to an identification with Jesus and often stopped
hearing the challenge presented to its own pride and
religiosity by what it called the "good news" of Jesus.

Every age of the church's life has seen new efforts to
proclaim the gospel and to hear the good news in new
situations. The church fathers (and some recently discovered "mothers"),[15] for example, tried to read the
Bible in the context of the problems and nascent heresies of the early church, using the tools of allegorical
interpretation current in both religious and secular
writings of their day. Later, Thomas Aquinas mediated
the encounter of church authority between the Biblical
story and the Greek scientific world view. Reformers
such as Luther and Calvin saw in the Bible a bulwark
against Roman tradition and tried to cut through inter-
vening centuries to recover a purely Biblical faith.

While it is easy for us to look back at these early
interpretations and recognize in them biases and distor-
tions, it is much harder for us to transcend the authority
of contemporary interpretations. The scientific world
view and method of study have had a profound impact
on Biblical study in the last century. New standards for
historical accuracy and linguistic precision have led
scholars to a much clearer picture of what the Bible
meant when it was written and even what may have
been the events behind the story. It is impossible to
overestimate the liberating power of the historical-critical method as applied to the study of the Bible. There
was for the first time a way to look behind the traditions
at the stories themselves that faith claimed as authorita-

tive. There was and is still a method of dealing with the text that recognizes its historical context but helps to overcome the obstacles of language, literary form, history, and culture that separate us from its origins. "Descriptive Biblical theology," which relies on the tools of historical and literary criticism, is still the dominant mode for doing Biblical study, and no responsible scholar today denies its importance.[16]

Increasingly, however, scholars are saying that the scientific, critical method by itself is not enough. In 1957, Rudolf Bultmann issued a challenge to those claiming the validity of scientific method as a means to arrive at objective truth.[17] More than a decade earlier, Dietrich Bonhoeffer's unfinished essay on telling the truth[18] introduced a concern that greater attention be paid to the historical situation of the interpreter and the biases inherent in it. Again, the Biblical theology movement and its current crisis, which was brought to scholars' attention by Brevard Childs[19] and discussed further by James Barr and Van A. Harvey,[20] pose the question of the relationship between faith concerns and scientific investigation, of the meaning and thrust of the Biblical story as a whole. More recently, a growing appreciation of the role of language and image, language as event and the intersection of aesthetics and methodology, is pushing Biblical scholars to look more closely at the broader field of hermeneutics as it relates to literature, the arts, and the social setting for insight into how meaning is communicated.[21] In yet different ways, Dorothee Soelle[22] and José Miranda[23] have forcefully raised the question of the social valence of the Biblical story and the political and economic context in which the Bible was written and is read. Another interdisciplinary approach to Biblical study incorporates insights

from depth psychology, exploring the connection between the Biblical story and human transformation.[24]
Finally, women and men writing on liberation theology
have brought to the work of Biblical study a commitment to an "engagement" style of working that might
be called an action/reflection model (Russell), a unity of
theory and praxis (Soelle), or a critical reflection on
praxis (Gutiérrez).[25] By whatever name it is called, this
method brings both contemporary self-understanding
and the lived experience of the reader deliberately and
actively into the interaction and encounter between
reader and text.

The effect of these influences on Biblical study is to
make this an exciting time of transition and ferment in
the field. It seems to be what Thomas Kuhn calls a time
of "paradigm shift,"[26] when even the methods used and
the questions asked of a field of study are changing. It
is a time when new models for working may be tenta-
tively suggested and tested out as ways to live within
those changes. In the case of Biblical study, it is a time
when we must be developing new ways to "translate"
or carry over meaning as well as information between
the different worlds of Biblical writers and contemporary people, so that God's liberating Word can still be
heard and proclaimed. Without pretending to have
found the only answer to how to proceed, I will suggest
some of the assumptions or presuppositions that guide
my own study and that may provide a beginning from
which we can look not only at the texts suggested in the
subsequent chapters of this book but also at other passages requiring our attention as we meet the Bible with
our own questions of identity and life-style that can
bear and even demand the risk of liberation.

IV. *A Proposed Model for Biblical Interpretation*

The assumptions with which I come to the process of Biblical interpretation can be grouped into four areas. They do not represent four sequential steps through which I progress to a final conclusion, but rather four perspectives through which I continue to return— somewhat in a spiraling fashion—so that the new insights gained at any point in the process are tested against the requirements of the other perspectives. For that reason, work on any given text is never finished, but only provisionally summarized at points along the way.

The first assumption is of *the "alien" nature of the texts of the Scriptures.* By their language, world view, and the social and historical situations in which they developed, they are foreign to me as a woman living in contemporary America. The methods of historical and literary criticism are demanded, then, in order to allow the texts their own objective reality and integrity and yet to recover an understanding of what happened, and, more importantly, what that meant to the authors and their communities. The approach of canonical criticism is also important because it provides insight into the traditions to which a particular author referred in order to recognize, understand, and interpret the contemporary situation, and insight into the way in which *that* event in turn was read by later interpreters as "authoritative" tradition pointing to the activities of God and God's people.

Whatever historical information we can recover about the authors and the situations in which they wrote, the common ground that we share is the text itself. The "event" of experience structured and expressed in language that is found in a passage of Scripture needs also to be allowed its world-building function as an artistic creation (which sets apart a piece of reality into a "world" of specific shape, colors, dimensions, and perspectives). Hence, a second part of the task of Biblical study is *seeing how the data of reality are put together*—what pattern of action or what argument is set forth, how its points of emphasis are highlighted, what causal connections are implied, what theological or other issues are raised, how human relationships are reordered or shown in a new light, etc. Language as event—that is, turned to the task of world-building—is not simply the univocal language of technology or of information, which needs only to be explained, but it becomes "multivocal"[27] and needs to be *understood* through an encounter or intersection of the world it embodies with the world of the reader. Such a meeting is invariably a mutual examining or questioning of reader and text, which demands a response from the reader. In the case of the texts of Scripture, the response at stake is the two-sided one of faith and active response.

Both because of their ability as artistic creations to confront the world of the reader with a new world, and because of the subject matter with which they deal, the texts of Scripture are anthropological. They are human stories and thus implicate human beings in them. They are not stories of the cavortings of gods on a plane parallel to ours (and so by definition never touching it), but rather stories of how a people has understood its relationship to God as worked out through history and through a recovery of the ground rules of that relationship implied in the stories of how it all began. Insofar as these are human stories, then, despite the distance of their origin from the contemporary situation, I as reader am never completely separate from them. Insofar as I identify with and claim their story as my own, it is part of me, and I have set myself up for questioning by it as well as offering questions to it. A third assumption in the process of Biblical interpretation is thus *the common humanity of the reader and the text.*

There are at least two implications of this presupposition for the process of Biblical study. First, because human existence is social existence—and, furthermore, because the texts themselves have their original locus in the community that gathered and preserved them—a group or corporate context seems to yield the most fruitful studies of the Biblical texts. This does not imply any diminishing of the task of scholarly investigation, but rather its enrichment as it is filtered through the lenses of varied human experiences and technical skills by means of a sustained conversation. (Although I would never suggest that the church is the only or even the best place for such work to go on, the implications seem clear that *at least* in the context of the church and its congregations, Biblical study ought to be taking place.)

The second implication of the common humanity of reader and text is that a part of the total process of interpretation involves the reader's entering into the story primarily through its human characters—the psalmist who is praying, for example, or the various people in the story of the healing at the pool by the Sheep Gate, which is told in John, ch. 5—not by pretending to reenter the ancient situation, but by finding their experiences and attitudes in herself or himself. (In its most sophisticated form, such archaeology of the subject is what happens in psychotherapy.) If in this step the reader is honest about her or his own attitudes and those parts of the self which find kinship with the roles, relationships, and experiences described in the text, then this process could be the first step in the kind of ideological criticism that Soelle sees as crucial in allowing the traditional methodologies their full creative power and in beginning to forge a political theology.

This perception of what happens in the process of encountering the text leads me to my fourth assumption, which is really my point of departure, namely, *the faith understanding that I bring to the text.* Thus, the God to whose Word I am trying to listen through the medium of the text is one I might describe in an Old Testament metaphor as a God who is always to be found a day's journey *ahead* of the most advanced of God's people and yet *in the midst* of them; a God whose bias is with the poor and dispossessed; and a God who finds a locus for power in human powerlessness. This God can never be captured in any human definition or job description, or even any combination of them. It is a God who calls into question every human self-understanding with a new option for both understanding and behavior (faith and praxis). This new option can be summarized as the word event of the new creation, which must constantly be known anew in each situation, and of which the proleptic or anticipatory experience in human terms is the experience of liberation.

2

INTERPRETING
PATRIARCHAL TRADITIONS
Elisabeth Schüssler Fiorenza

The Hebrew and Christian Scriptures originated in a patriarchal society and perpetuated the androcentric (male-centered) traditions of their culture. Today, feminist analyses have uncovered the detrimental effects of these traditions on women's self-understanding and role in society and in the churches. Christians, both women and men, consequently face a grave dilemma. On the one hand they seek to remain faithful to the life-giving truth of the Biblical revelation and on the other hand they seek to free themselves from all patriarchal traditions and sexist concepts that hinder their human and Christian liberation. The interpretation and understanding of the androcentric traditions of the Bible is therefore a major theological task for all Christians today. This task cannot be accomplished by putting down the feminist critique as "unscholarly," "somewhat uninformed," or "excessive,"[28] but only by taking seriously the fact that the Hebrew and Christian Scriptures share in the concepts and ideologies of their patriarchal culture and age.

In order to accomplish this task we have to take into account the methods of historical-critical scholarship,

the results of the discussion of methods of interpretation, and the insights of the feminist analysis.[29] Historical-critical scholarship has taught us that it is necessary
to understand the historical setting, the cultural environment, the literary forms, and the specific language
of a text if we interpret and teach or preach the Bible.
Discussion of interpretation has underlined that a val-
ue-free, objectivistic historiography is a scholarly
fiction. All interpretation of texts depends upon the
presuppositions, intellectual interests, politics, or preju-
dices of the interpreter, historian, or theologian. Scholars are always committed, whether they realize it or
not. Feminist analyses have, therefore, pointed out that
the Biblical texts were not only recorded from an androcentric point of view but were also consciously or
unconsciously interpreted by exegetes and preachers
from a perspective of cultural male dominance. Several
Biblical texts that were throughout the centuries
quoted to support women's inferiority and submission
do not have in their original intent and context a mis-
ogynist slant. The study of androcentric traditions in the
Bible has thus to observe not only the original intention
of the texts but also their androcentric history of interpretation. Biblical history, just like history on the whole,
has become "his story"[30] recorded and interpreted
from an androcentric point of view.

  This chapter discusses a sampling of patriarchal texts
and androcentric interpretations of the Bible in order
to demonstrate how a reading of the Bible from a feminist perspective could contribute to a better and deeper
understanding of the Biblical message. Insofar as this
discussion singles out for interpretation androcentric
and patriarchal Scriptural texts, it might appear at first
glance one-sided and overly critical. Insofar as it uncov-

ers sexist presuppositions and biases of modern exegetes and preachers, it will provoke emotional reaction and controversy. Yet such a study might also recover in some seemingly androcentric texts a tacit criticism and transcendence of patriarchal and androcentric values. Moreover, a feminist interpretation can show that some texts, even though recorded from an androcentric perspective, refer to a historical situation in which women had more authority and influence than is usually attributed to them.

I. *Androcentric Traditions of the Old Testament*[31]

Although some texts of the Old Testament might reflect a matriarchal or matrilineal society, the patriarchal character of Hebrew culture is undisputed. Spanning nearly a millennium and embracing a variety of religio-cultural contexts, the Hebrew Scriptures clearly espouse male priority and superiority in the national as well as in the religious community.

Patriarchal Texts. Israel as a nation and as a religious community was constituted by male-dominated families, and full membership in it was reserved to the adult male. It is true that Israel had this patriarchal fabric in common with all the surrounding Near Eastern cultures and religions. Yet the legal and social position of women was often lower in Israel than in the neighboring countries.[32] In the Hebrew patriarchal society, women were totally dependent on their fathers and husbands. Numbers 30:2–12, for example, demonstrates the complete dependency and subordination of a daughter or a wife, not only in familial-cultural affairs but also in religious matters. The vows of a daughter or

a wife were not considered valid if the father or the
husband vetoed them.

> But when her husband makes them null and void
> on the day that he hears them, then whatever pro-
> ceeds out of her lips concerning her vows, or con-
> cerning her pledge of herself, shall not stand: her
> husband has made them void, and the Lord will
> forgive her. (Num. 30:12.)

The main values of Hebrew patriarchal society were
the perpetuation of the family and the clan, as well as
the protection of property. Since sons prolonged the
family line and preserved the family's fortunes, they
were highly desired. Daughters were less valued, because they would leave the family when they married.
A daughter was the property of her father and could
even be sold as a slave if the purchaser intended to
make her his own or his son's concubine (Lev. 21:7–11).
In early Hebrew society the future husband had to pay
a bride-price as a compensation to the bride's family.
Well known in this regard is the story of Leah and
Rachel (Gen. 29:16–30), who complained that their father, after having sold them, had used the money paid
for them (Gen. 31:15). Less known but even more dras-
tic is the story of David, Saul, and Michal (I Sam. 18:
20–27).

That a daughter was completely at the disposal of her
father is apparent in the story of Lot and his daughters.
In Gen. 19:1–11[33] two strangers accept the invitation of
Lot to stay in his home. When the men of the town want
to abuse them sexually, Lot offers his own daughters
instead:

> Behold, I have two daughters who have not known
> man; let me bring them out to you, and do to them

> as you please; only do nothing to these men, for
> they have come under the shelter of my roof.
> (Gen.19:8.)

Although the daughters are not ravished, the sacred-
ness of hospitality is clearly the greater value in the
story. The incident cannot be explained as an example
of "bargaining by the unacceptable alternative," in
which the offer is so shocking that no one would dream
of accepting it. This becomes apparent when we consider the very similar tale in Judg. 19:22–30. As in Gen.
19:1–11, a father offers his virgin daughter and his
guest's concubine to the men of the town for sexual
abuse in order to protect the male guest of his house.
When the men did not listen to him, the guest "seized
his concubine, and put her out to them; and they knew
her, and abused her all night until the morning" (Judg.
19:25). Because the woman dies from their violence,
Israel rallies to warfare against the offending town of
the Benjaminites, "for they have committed abomina-
tion and wantonness in Israel" (Judg. 20:6). However,
there is uttered no word of criticism of the husband who
saved his own life by offering his concubine for rape and
abuse.

The extent to which women were in the power of
men is also demonstrated in the conclusion of this narrative cycle. After the Israelites have defeated the Benjaminites, they feel compassion for them.

> One tribe is cut off from Israel this day. What shall
> we do for wives of those who are left, since we have
> sworn by the Lord that we will not give them any
> of our daughters as wives? (Judg. 21:6–7.)

When the congregation finds out that no one from Ja-
besh-gilead had taken this oath, they decide to kill all

inhabitants of the city except for four hundred virgins whom they gave as wives to the surviving Benjaminites (Judg. 21:12). Since there were still some men without wives, the elders of the congregation decide to obtain more women through "highway" robbery. When, at the occasion of the yearly festival, the daughters of Shiloh came out to dance in the vineyards, the Benjaminites abducted them, and the elders of Israel were prepared to defend this action against the complaining fathers or brothers of the women (Judg. 21:20–23). The virgin daughters are clearly the possession of their fathers. The women themselves have nothing to say throughout all these events. Just as at the beginning of the narrative cycle hospitality was more highly valued than the lives of women, so at the end the survival of the tribe of Benjamin justifies the brutal violence against them.[34]

In a patriarchal family structure the daughter is dependent upon her father or brother and the wife becomes totally dependent upon her husband. Thus, the woman remains all her life a minor. The Decalogue includes a man's wife among his possessions, along with his house and land, his male and female slaves, his ox and his ass (Ex. 20:17; Deut. 5:21). The root meaning of the Hebrew verb "to marry a wife" is "to become master" (ba'al, cf. Deut. 21:13; 24:4). The wife, therefore, calls her husband master (ba'al, cf. Ex. 21:4, 22; II Sam. 11:26) and lord ('adōn, Gen. 18:12; Judg. 19:26; Amos 4:1). Even after the wife is widowed, her father-in-law retains authority over her. (Gen. 38:24.) The wife's primary task in life is to bear children, and her greatest honor is motherhood. Barrenness was, therefore, seen as misfortune and divine punishment (Gen. 11:30; 30:1; Ex. 23:26; I Sam. 1:6; Hos. 9:14).[35] In Hebrew society, polygyny was legally recognized, the husband could take a concubine, and divorce was a male prerogative (Deut. 24:1–4). Whereas woman's sexual misconduct was severely punished, infidelity on the part of the man was penalized only if he violated the rights of another man. Since sexual intercourse with a betrothed virgin or a married woman offended the property rights of the patriarch, it was severely punished and provoked even Yahweh's intervention. A good example is the story of Abraham and Sarah, which we find with variations three times in Genesis: Gen. 12:10 to 13:1;20:1–18;26:6–11 (Isaac and Rebekah).

According to the Yahwist's (J) account (Gen.12:10 to 13:1), in order to save his own life Abraham persuades his beautiful wife Sarah to pass as his sister in Egypt. She is taken into the harem of Pharaoh, but Yahweh intervenes on her behalf. Pharaoh reproaches Abraham for not telling him the truth and extradicts him and his company. The Yahwist's account tells the marvelous preservation of the future mother of the heir of promise. Abraham is at fault.

Even though location and names are different, the Elohist's (E) story (Gen. 20:1–18) materially corresponds in detail to the Yahwistic account. Yet the story clearly now has a different theological tendency. The author takes pains to justify, theologically, Abraham's selfish action. This androcentric shift becomes clear from the following points: First, Yahweh has to castigate Abimelech because Sarah is another man's wife (v.3). Abraham's property rights are violated. Second, the story stresses that Sarah herself says that she is the sister of Abraham (v.5). Third, it is emphasized that Abimelech does not touch Sarah (v.6c). Fourth, Abraham justifies himself, giving as his motive theological reasons

("There is no fear of God at all in this place," v.11b). Fifth, Sarah is indeed Abraham's sister because they have the same father, but a different mother (vs. 12, 16). Finally, Abimelech takes care to honor Abraham, to restore Sarah to him, and to vindicate her publicly. Abraham in turn prays for Abimelech and his house, and the wrath of Yahweh is taken from them. The Elohist's story thus glorifies Abraham and exonerates King Abimelech. Sarah comes into view solely as Abraham's compliant wife who remained untouched by another man because of Yahweh's intervention on behalf of her husband's rights. The story clearly exhibits patriarchal values and pictures its characters from an androcentric point of view.

In prophetic times, the patriarchal marriage relationship becomes theologized insofar as it becomes a model for the covenant relationshp between Yahweh and Israel. This theological model not only divinely authorizes the superiority of the husband but also theologically sanctions the inferior role of women in the patriarchal marriage relationship. Further, the image of the marriage between Yahweh and Israel eliminates female imagery and symbolism from the divine realm insofar as Yahweh has no divine female consort but only a human bride to love and to serve him.[36] The oracle of salvation in Hosea 2:19 does not project divine equality between Yahweh and Israel for the future, but solely announces that "Israel will not just respect Yahweh somewhat reluctantly, since he is its legal lord, but it knows itself to be placed into a completely new, loving relationship with him."[37]

The prophets, moreover, often use the image of Israel or Jerusalem as a woman or wife in a negative way in order to censure Israel for its apostasy to the cults and

mythologies of Canaan. Through the marriage metaphor, Israel's apostasy and idolatry become identified
with the adultery, fornication, and whoredom of
women. This theological language and imagery associ-
ates women not only with sexual misconduct but also
with unfaithfulness and idolatry.

> Plead with your mother, plead—
>   for she is not my wife,
>   and I am not her husband—
> that she put away her harlotry from her face,
>   and her adultery from between her breasts;
> lest I strip her naked
>   and make her as in the day she was born.
>
> (Hos. 2:2–3.)

The theological image of Yahweh as the loving husband
and Israel as the unfaithful wife has in the history of
theology perpetuated the subordinate role of women
and associated them with whoredom and adultery as
well as with apostasy and idolatry.

Androcentric Interpretation. The Yahwistic creation
story, Gen., chs. 2,3, is an example used throughout
Christian history by theologians and preachers both to
teach that woman is according to God's intention deriv-
ative from man and to characterize her as the temptress
of man and the one through whom sin came into the
world.[38] More recent feminist studies, however, have
convincingly shown that, far from being "sexist," the
Genesis story maintains the co-equalness of woman and
man, although Gen. 2:18 clearly indicates that the story
is told from the male point of view since *'ādām* in Gen.,
ch. 2, not only is a generic term but also communicates
that the first individual human being was male.[39]

The narrative follows an ancient pattern of creation myths in which the gods at first attempt a trial creation before they accomplish the perfect creation.[40] The creation of the animals follows this trial-creation pattern insofar as the animals are not co-equal beings with *'ād-ām*. Only the woman who is taken from *'ādām* is co-equal with him and the perfect creation. The linguistic consonance of the terms "man" *('īsh)* and "woman" *('ishsha)* underlines this co-equality. The statement of the narrator in Gen. 2:24 summarizes the intention of the creation story (Gen. 2:4b–24). It explains that man leaves his parents in order to become one flesh with a woman. This summarizing statement of the Yahwist interestingly enough does not presuppose the patriarchal family model, according to which the woman leaves her family to become part of the male clan, but states exactly the opposite.

As Gen. 2:4b–24 attempts to explain the co-equalness and unity of man and woman in marriage, so Gen., ch. 3, attempts to come to terms with Israel's experience of the oppressive human reality in which man and woman find themselves. Along with ch. 2, the narrative in ch. 3 forms a unit that is not prescriptive, but is a story that tries to make sense out of man's and woman's present existence. It explains why woman lives now under patriarchy and suffers from childbearing, and why man has to toil and wrestle his livelihood from the earth from which he is taken. Whereas before the Fall the husband left his family to become one flesh with his wife, now the woman is tied into a relationship of domination by her desire for her husband. In consequence of this desire, her childbearing increases and, moreover, causes her great pain and suffering. The penalties in ch. 3: 14–19 reflect the culturally conditioned situation of man and woman in a nomadic and agricultural society. Man's domination of woman is a consequence of sin and transgression. Yahweh did not intend this patriarchal domination of woman, but had created her as co-equal to man.

The Priestly writer (P) grasped this point of the Yahwistic creation account when he summarized God's intention in the creation of humans:

God created humankind *('ādām)* in his own image . . . ; male *(zākār)* and female *(neqēbā)* he created them. (Gen. 1:27.)

Far from being the androcentric or sexist story as it is often misunderstood, the Yahwistic creation account implies a criticism of the patriarchal relationship between man and woman. The domination of the wife by the husband is interpreted as a consequence of sin.

Androcentric Traditioning. If we wish to understand Biblical texts, we have not only to ask whether a tradition of androcentric interpretation has veiled their original intention but also to question whether the original narrator or author in an androcentric way has told history that was not androcentric at all. A good example of such a male-centered tradition process is, in my opinion, provided by the scattered references to the prophet Miriam. Exegetes generally agree that Miriam originally was an independent leader in Israel and was made a sister of Aaron and Moses only in the later traditions of the Old Testament (cf. Num. 26:59 [P]). According to Ex. 15:20 (J), Miriam was a prophet who proclaimed the triumph of Yahweh over the Egyptian Pharaoh. Her song is the oldest extant praise of Yahweh in the Old Testament. The prophetic tradition knows

Miriam as a leader of Israel during the exodus, co-equal with Moses and Aaron (Micah 6:4). Numbers 20:1 mentions Kadesh as her burial place.

Numbers, ch 12 (JE), represents one of the oldest and most interesting traditions on Miriam. The text does not yet know that Miriam, Aaron, and Moses are siblings. The story begins with the rebellion of Miriam and Aaron against the superiority and authority of Moses. They not only reproach Moses for having married a non-Israelite wife but they also maintain that Yahweh has not revealed things solely through Moses: "Has the Lord indeed spoken only through Moses? Has he not spoken through us also?" With these words, Miriam and Aaron claim to be equal with Moses as recipients and mediators of divine revelation. The rest of the story is told in order to reject this claim of Miriam and Aaron. The narrative not only betrays a bias for Moses but also repudiates Miriam much more severely than Aaron. Whereas the text mentions Miriam first, as leader of the rebellion, the answer of Yahweh addresses first Aaron and then Miriam (v. 5). Yahweh stresses that Moses is the authentic revelation bearer to whom God speaks "mouth to mouth, clearly, and not in dark speech" (v. 8). Although the speech of Yahweh is described as first addressing Aaron and Miriam, the Lord punishes Miriam but not Aaron. The punishment of the rebellious woman is the main theme of this androcentric text. The narrative stresses her dependence on the goodwill of Aaron and Moses. When she is afflicted with leprosy (cf. also Deut. 24:9), Aaron begs Moses to intercede and Moses prays for her to God. Yet Yahweh behaves like a stern patriarch. Miriam is punished in the same way as if she were a girl whose "father had but spit in her face." Therefore, she is "shamed seven days" (v. 14). The story clearly establishes Moses' superiority and accords Miriam the same relationship to Yahweh as a girl had in a patriarchal family. The narrative, however, presupposes the knowledge that Miriam competed with Moses for the prophetic leadership of Israel and argues against such an aspiration by a woman.

In dealing with this story of an "uppity woman," modern male commentators are helpless. They speculate about jealousy between siblings[41] or the displeasure of the "prima donna" of the women's choir[42] over God's preference for Moses. Even such a scholar as Martin Noth[43] attempts to explain away Miriam's exceptional role by asserting that as the only female figure around Moses she led the case against the Cushite women, but in claiming equal prophetic status with Moses she was only following Aaron. According to Noth, the point of the story is the mild punishment of Miriam, who actually should have been afflicted with permanent leprosy for revolting against the great servant of Yahweh. Just like the first recorder, so modern commentators on the story cannot conceive of Miriam as an independent leader in Israel, but only as the jealous and rebellious sister of Moses with whom Yahweh deals as a patriarchal father would handle his uppity daughter. The story of Miriam's rebellion in its present form functions to repudiate Miriam's leadership claim and to extol Moses' superiority. A careful reading of the story, however, detects elements of a tradition which knew that Miriam was a leading figure in Israel's past.

With these few examples I have attempted to show that a feminist reading of various Old Testament texts uncovers their patriarchal and androcentric character. Yet such an interpretation can also liberate Biblical texts from an androcentric bias and misunderstanding by demonstrating that certain narratives, which are often misunderstood by an androcentric interpretation, indirectly protest against their patriarchal cultural values (cf. Gen., chs. 2, 3), or that they reflect a stage in the tradition that was relatively free from such a bias (cf. Gen., ch. 12). Such a feminist reading might furthermore be able to recover traces of the lost "her-story" of great women in the Old Testament.

II.   *Androcentric Traditions in the New Testament*[44]

It is quite remarkable that the canonical literature of the New Testament does not transmit a single androcentric statement or sexist story of Jesus, although he lived and preached in a patriarchal culture and society.[45] Studies of the sociocultural conditions of the early Christian movement have shown that it was a socially and religiously deviant group similar to other sectarian groups in the Judaism of the first century. In distinction to the sect of Qumran or the Pharisees, for instance, the Jesus movement was not an exclusive, but an inclusive, group. Jesus did not call into his fellowship righteous, pious, and highly esteemed persons but invited tax collectors, sinners, and women to be his followers and friends. He rejected the primacy of the Jewish cultic purity laws and therefore could include in his community of disciples the outlaws and nonpersons of the Jewish religion and society. In the fellowship of Jesus, women apparently did not play a marginal role, even though only a few references to women disciples have survived the androcentric tradition and redaction process of the gospels.

Women accompanied Jesus as disciples in his ministry in Galilee, Judea, and Jerusalem (Mark 15:40 and parallels) and witnessed his execution as a criminal on the cross. They were not afraid to be known as his followers. Moreover, women were, according to all criteria of historical authenticity, the first witnesses of the resurrection, for this fact could not have been derived from contemporary Judaism or invented by the primitive church. That the tradition did not leave these women disciples anonymous, but identified them by name, suggests that they played an important role in the Christian group in Palestine. Their most outstanding leader appears to have been Mary Magdalene,[46] since all four Gospels transmit her name, whereas the names of the other women vary. Thus, according to the Gospel traditions, women were the primary apostolic witnesses for the fundamental data of the early Christian message: they were the witnesses of Jesus' ministry, his death, his burial, and his resurrection.

A closer examination of the Gospel accounts, however, discloses the androcentric tendency to play down the women's roles as witnesses and apostles of the Easter event. This trend is apparent in Mark's Gospel, which stresses that the women "said nothing to any one, for they were afraid" (Mark 16:8). It is also evident in Luke's comment that the words of the women seemed to the Eleven and those with them "an idle tale, and they did not believe them," but instead went to see for themselves (Luke 24:11). In Acts 1:21, Luke excludes the apostleship of women when he stresses that only a man was eligible to replace Judas. This androcentric bias is also reflected in the Lucan confessional statement: "The Lord has risen indeed, and has appeared to Simon!" (Luke 24:34). This Lucan androcentric confessional formula corresponds to that of the pre-Pauline creedal tradition quoted in I Cor. 15:3 ff. which men-

tions Cephas and the Eleven as the principal witnesses
of the resurrection, but does not refer to the witness of
the women.[47] The androcentric proclivity to play down
the first witness of the resurrection by women is also
apparent in the editing of the Fourth Gospel, which
takes pains to ensure that the beloved disciple, not
Mary Magdalene, was the first believer in the resurrection (John 20: 1–18). Most contemporary commentators
show the same androcentric inclination to suppress the
significance of the women as primary witnesses to the
resurrection when they stress that their witness had
only a preliminary function, since according to Jewish
law women were not competent to witness.

Patriarchalization of the Early Church. Scholars generally agree that Jesus did not leave his followers a blue-
print for the organization and structuring of the Christian church. In Paul's time, leadership roles were still
diversified and based on charismatic authority. The process of solidification and institutionalization set in only
gradually during the last part of the first century. The
pastoral epistles provide evidence that the Christian
community and its offices were perceived and patterned after the patriarchal family structures of the
time. Church authority was vested in elders, deacons,
and bishops. Criteria for their election from the male
members of the community were that they must be
husbands of one wife and must have demonstrated their
ability to rule the community by the proper ordering of
their households and the successful upbringing of their
children (I Tim. 3:1–13; Titus 1:5–9).

From a sociological perspective, the gradual institutionalization and adaption of the Christian movement to
the patriarchal societal structures of the time was un-

avoidable if the Christian community was to expand and to survive. At the same time, this structural solidification meant a patriarchalization of the Christian leadership functions that gradually eliminated women from roles of leadership and relegated them to subordinate feminine roles. The more Christianity became a genuine part of the patriarchal Jewish or Greco-Roman society and culture, the more it had to relegate women's leadership to fringe groups or to limit it to women's functions. In gnostic as well as catholic groups, "maleness" became the standard for being a full Christian. The recently discovered Coptic Gospel of Thomas states:

> Simon Peter said to them [the disciples]: Let Mary [Magdalene] go away from us, for women are not worthy of life. Jesus said: Lo, I shall lead her so that I may make her a male, that she too may become a living spirit, resembling you males. For every woman who makes herself a male will enter the kingdom of heaven. (Log. 114.)

The androcentric emphasis of the Pauline tradition stresses the subordination of women on theological grounds and reflects the reactionary patriarchal evolution of the Christian community. Whether or not Paul himself initiated this patriarchal reaction is discussed by scholars.[48] Certainly, however, the theological justification of the patriarchalization of the Christian community expressed in I Cor. 11:2–16 and 14:33b–36 was able to claim the authority of Paul without being challenged.

In the context of his discussion of Christian enthusiasts Paul addresses, in his first letter to the Corinthians, the question of women's behavior in the Christian congregation. In both cases when Paul speaks about women he is concerned not with women's rights or the role of women in the church in general but with their concrete behavior in the Christian worship assembly in Corinth. In I Cor. 11:2–16, Paul does not deny that women can prophesy; he only demands that they should be appropriately dressed. In this debate, Paul adduces different arguments that he derived from nature, custom, and Scripture. According to Paul, the order of creation is hierarchical: God–Christ–Man–Woman (v. 3). The Corinthian women still live in this order of creation and they ought to behave accordingly (vs. 4–6). Verse 7 theologically justifies the inferiority and dependence of woman: Man is the image and glory of God, whereas woman is only the glory of man, a prolongation and manifestation of his authority and power. With his reference to Gen. 2:18–23 in vs. 8–9, Paul demonstrates that man is prior to woman in the order of creation, and in v. 10 he adduces a further theological argument, namely, the presence of the angels in the worship assembly. Verses 11–12 assert that Paul does not wish to negate the reciprocity of man and woman in Christ. Yet, at stake in the Corinthian discussion is not the theological co-equality of Christian women and men but the propriety of women's conduct (vs. 13–15). In his last sentence, Paul points to the universal practice of the churches and to his own apostolic authority. It is clear that for him the issue is one of contentiousness and party spirit (v. 16).

Similarly, the passage I Cor. 14:33b–36, which is widely held to be a post-Pauline interpolation, addresses the question of order and competition within the community (cf. v. 40). For the sake of order, I Cor. 14:33b–36 explicitly forbids women to speak in the assembly and directs them to their husbands for religious instruction. The main argument here is decency: "For it is shameful for a woman to speak in church."

The so-called household codes of the later Pauline literature uphold the patriarchal family order of the time and therefore demand the subordination of the wife to the husband. Their rules of conduct for women, children, and slaves are not specifically Christian, but are a part of the Jewish and Greco-Roman culture of the time.[49] These culturally conditioned injunctions are, however, in Ephesians theologized or, better, Christologized, so that the model after which the Christian patriarchal marriage ought to be patterned is the relationship between Christ and the church. It is true that the husbands are admonished to imitate Christ's love for the church in their love of their wives. Nevertheless, the author does not demand equal love and subordination of husband and wife, but decidedly preserves the patriarchal order in a Christian context. Just as Christ loves the church, which is clearly subordinated to him, so a husband should love his wife, who is required to be subordinated to him in everything (Eph. 5:24) and to pay him his due respect (Eph. 5:33). The subordination of the wife to the husband is, as in I Cor., ch. 11, justified with the theological rationale that the husband is the head of the wife as Christ is the head of the church (Eph. 5:23).

The household code of I Peter 3:1–7 may be considered an extension of Pauline patriarchal emphasis, inasmuch as the first letter of Peter is widely considered to represent Pauline theology and tradition. The author points to the example of the holy women of the Old Testament, especially of Sarah, in order to justify his stance that women best practice their Christian mission in submitting to the societal patriarchal order. In doing so, they might win over their husbands to Christianity without saying a word. The recommendation to the husbands in turn asks that they live considerately with

their wives and bestow honor unto them. The author
stresses that husband and wife are "joint heirs of the
grace of life," but considers woman to be the "weaker
vessel" (KJV). As elsewhere in the New Testament, the
term "weak" refers to physical, moral, or spiritual and
intellectual inferiority. The expression "vessel" deroga-
torily describes woman as an object. Since this mode of
characterizing woman is based on Jewish as well as Hel-
lenistic sentiment, the author maintains the natural
weakness of woman in accordance with the androcentric definitions of his time.

I Timothy 2:9–15 combines both the household code
tradition and the silence in church tradition of the Pauline androcentric emphasis. Concerned with the proper
behavior at worship, the author demands that men lift
up their hands when they pray and that women not
wear braided hair, jewelry, and expensive dress. They
are, moreover, to be quiet and to learn with all submis-
siveness. They may on no account presume to teach or
to have authority over men (v. 12). The author theologically justifies his androcentric injunctions with a reference to Gen., chs. 2 and 3: Eve is not only second in the
order of creation but she is also first in the order of sin.
Woman's task is childbearing, and her salvation is dependent on this task (v. 15). Christian women were to
conduct themselves according to contemporary patriarchal role definitions.

The author appears to formulate his patriarchal theology and ethics in order to counter the influence of a
rival Christian group. This group seems to have had
great success among women (II Tim. 3:6), probably because it accorded women teaching and leadership functions and did not limit them to their societal patriarchal
roles. In opposition to this Christian theological under-

standing of women's role, the author stresses that women are not to behave in an unusual way by wanting to teach or to have authority in the community. They are rather to be silent (stressed twice!), submissive, and modest.

Androcentric Traditioning. At the end of the first century A.D., a Christian prophet, who was the head of a prophetic group or school, exercised great leadership in the community of Thyatira (Rev. 2:19–23). The authority of this prophet must have been well established in the community, since the author of the book of Revelation criticizes the congregation for not having actively opposed her, and her influence must have been far-reaching and threatening to him. In labeling her "Jezebel" he insinuates that, like the Old Testament queen, the prophet promoted idolatry and achieved her goals through seductive power and malevolent scheming. The author characterizes her activity with language gleaned from the imagery and language of the Old Testament prophets describing the lapses of Israel into idolatry and apostasy as adultery, whoredom, and gross immorality. Despite this attack by the author of Revelation, the text still communicates that the prophet was not the head of an already heretic group, since she still exercised her leadership within the community of Thyatira.[50] Her impact must have been lasting, because Thyatira became in the second century a center of the Montanist movement in which female prophets were prominent (Epiphanius, Heresies 51.3).

Although we no longer know the real name of the prophet of Thyatira, the text of Revelation furnishes us with an example showing that even at the end of the first century women exercised prophetic leadership in the Christian community. In addition, this text provides a paradigm of how patriarchal and androcentric theologizing and polemics distorted the contribution of women in the early church. A feminist history of the first centuries of the Christian church could uncover the struggle between those women who were inspired by the Christian vision expressed in Gal. 3:28 and the androcentric leadership of the church that attempted to force Christian women back into their limited cultural, patriarchal roles.

III. *Suggestions for Interpreting Androcentric Texts of the Bible*

The methods for the interpretation of historical texts, as well as those of feminist studies, enable us to approach the androcentric passages of the Bible with the following insights and guidelines:

1. Historical texts have to be understood or evaluated in their historical setting, language, and form. Since the Biblical texts have their origin in a patriarchal culture, they reflect the androcentric situations, conditions, and values of this patriarchal culture. They appear to be, therefore, an excellent tool for the consciousness-raising of women and men in preaching and teaching.

2. Since Biblical texts are rooted in a patriarchal culture and recorded from an androcentric point of view, a careful analysis from a feminist perspective might unearth traces of a genuine "her-story" of women in the Bible. It is very important that teachers and preachers point out these instances of a genuine "her-story" again and again, so that women in the church become conscious of their own "her-story" in the Biblical patriarchal history.

3. Since Biblical androcentric texts are recorded and told from an patriarchal point of view, it will be helpful to retell the androcentric Biblical stories from the woman's point of view. As the Elohist retold the story of Abraham and Sarah from Abraham's point of view, so we should attempt to retell it from Sarah's perspective. An example of the retelling of Gen., chs. 2, 3, is Judith Plaskow's "The Coming of Lilith."[51] Such a retelling of Biblical stories is not a feminist invention. Throughout the centuries we have examples of parallel elaborations such as the apocryphal infancy stories or our Christmas legends.

4. Biblical texts are not only recorded but also translated and interpreted from a male perspective since most exegetes are not aware of the feminist perspective. We have therefore to be cautious in adopting standard scholarly interpretations of texts and to screen such interpretations for their androcentric or sexist presuppositions or prejudice.

5. Biblical revelation and truth about women are found, I would suggest, in those texts which transcend and criticize their patriarchal culture and religion. Such texts should be used to evaluate and to judge the patriarchal texts of the Bible. A Biblical interpretation which is concerned with the *meaning* of the Bible in a post-patriarchal culture has to maintain that solely the non-sexist traditions of the Bible present divine revelation if the Bible should not become a tool for the oppression of women. Such an interpretation does not suggest a "modernizing" of ancient texts,[52] but is a necessary corrective if we do not want to give the impression that we worship a sexist God and thus an idol who is made in the image of males.

3

IMAGES OF WOMEN

Joanna Dewey

Women in the Bible "appear for the most part simply as adjuncts of men, significant only in the context of men's activities."[53] Yet if we read the Bible afresh, watching particularly for stories and teachings concerning women, we shall find stories in which women are portrayed very positively in their own right, and teachings that reflect the equality of women and men. We may even find that there is a basic vision of free humankind in the Bible in which women and men are equal in their relationships with each other, with the world they live and act in, and with God.

In this chapter we shall look at and reread a few selected passages from the Old and the New Testaments in which the Bible transcends its patriarchal setting and portrays women in a positive light. Our purpose in doing so is threefold: first, simply to demonstrate that there are such passages in the Bible; second, to indicate some of the ways people have overlooked or explained away these passages; and third, and perhaps most important, to give examples of how to look at Biblical passages from a nonsexist or a feminist viewpoint.

No attempt has been made to give a comprehensive overview of images of women in the Bible. The passages do not even include some of the most important or outstanding sections, such as the creation stories (Gen., chs. 1;2), the story of Deborah (Judg., chs. 4;5), the portrayal of wisdom as a woman (Prov., chs. 8;9), the portrayal of the lovers in the Song of Solomon, or the story of Mary and Martha (Luke 10:38–42). Yet the passages selected help to show both a variety of positive images of women and a variety of ways such passages have been overlooked.

I. *Stories and Teachings from the Old Testament*

Exodus 1:15 to 2:10. [54] The faith of Israel was decisively shaped by the exodus event, the experience of deliverance from oppression in Egypt. The story of Moses and the Hebrew people in Egypt and their struggle toward freedom was central to Israel's faith because God's act of liberation was the basis of Israel's special relationship as a people chosen to serve God. And as some New Testament accounts begin with stories about the birth of Jesus Christ, the Redeemer (Matt. 1:18 to 2:23; Luke, chs. 1;2), so the exodus account begins with the story of the birth of Moses, an instrument for God's redemption of Israel.

The Hebrews were then an oppressed class in Egypt. The Pharaoh, the king of Egypt, felt threatened by their numbers and tried in succession three policies to decrease or wipe out the Hebrew people (Ex. 1:8–22). First, he subjected them to forced labor. When that failed, he commanded the two Hebrew midwives, Shiphrah and Puah, to dispose of all male Hebrew children at birth. If only the daughters survived, they could have been absorbed into the Egyptian people as slave wives. Shiphrah and Puah, however, "feared God" (vs. 17, 21). Therefore, they courageously disobeyed Pharaoh and permitted the male children to live.[55] So finally Pharaoh gave an open command to his people to drown all male Hebrew infants in the Nile.

At this point the birth story proper begins. A Hebrew woman bears a son. In an attempt to evade Pharaoh's command, the mother then prepares a basket to protect the baby and places the baby in the basket at the bank of the Nile. We are not told whether the father assists, approves, or even knows of his wife's actions. The baby is found by a daughter of Pharaoh, who, in disobedience to her father, rescues him, has him nursed by his own mother, and then brings him up as her own son in Pharaoh's house, naming him Moses. The boy survives to become the deliverer of his people.

Commentators generally ignore the crucial role that women played at the birth of Moses. They may note the wit of the midwives' reply to Pharaoh: that they could not carry out his order because the Hebrew women were so healthy that they bore their children before the midwives could get there (Ex. 1:19). In discussing the birth of Moses, they rightly point out the similarities of the story to the legendary motif of the exposed infant who is rescued by some human or divine agent. A legend about King Sargon's birth tells of his being set afloat in a basket on the Euphrates River. He is rescued, however, by a male peasant. On the whole, commentators simply take the women in the story for granted. They consider it natural for women to be concerned with birth and children.

Yet, if we look at the story of the women directly, rather than simply as a prelude to the story of Moses and the exodus, we find they are important in their own right and also have a theological significance. Certainly in both the story about the midwives and the story of the women's rescue of the baby, the women are acting independently and not as adjuncts of men.

In both stories the actions of the women are actions of disobedience to the authority of the Pharaoh. The midwives, Shiphrah and Puah, disobeyed explicitly because they feared God. The baby's mother and sister and Pharaoh's daughter act, according to the story, out of concern for the child, yet their concern caused them to disobey the male overlord. And in both stories the disobedience results in deliverance: The disobedience of the midwives saves the Hebrew people; the disobedience of the mother, sister, and Pharaoh's daughter saves Moses. "As the first to defy the oppressor, women alone take the initiative that leads to deliverance."[56]

And if God was later acting through Moses to deliver the people, then God first of all acted through these women to deliver the people. Women as well as men are God's agents of salvation and, in the story of the exodus, God's first agents.

II Kings 22:1 to 23: 3. In the preceding passage we reread the stories of the midwives and the women concerned with the birth of Moses. In doing so, we found that the women were the central characters of these stories, bringing about the deliverance of Israel. All that was necessary to see this was, first, to assume that women are fully human and that importance can therefore be attributed to their actions; and, second, to reread the story from the point of view of the women involved rather than of the men.

In the passage we are going to look at now concerning Huldah, the prophet, we hardly even need to do any retelling. Rather, we need to remember and reclaim as part of our history that women were prophets and were readily accepted as such throughout the Old and the New Testament. God spoke through women as well as men.

Josiah was king of Judah in the latter part of the seventh century B.C. During the beginning of his reign, and for some years before that, the Kingdom of Judah had been a vassal state of the Assyrian Empire. This meant not only that Judah had to pay tribute to the Assyrians but also that cults of Assyrian gods had to be practiced in the Jerusalem Temple, the house of the Lord. Assyria's power was crumbling, however, so that by about 625 B.C. Judah was in fact a free country again. Repairs were begun on the Temple. In the process of the repairs, a book of the Law was found. Scholars agree that the book consisted of some portion of our present book of Deuteronomy. The book was read to the king, who was greatly distressed, "for great is the wrath of the Lord that is kindled against us, because our fathers have not obeyed the words of this book" (II Kings 22:13). The king sent to "inquire of the Lord," that is, ask a prophet if the book was true. The prophet replied, "Thus says the Lord, Behold, I will bring evil upon this place and upon its inhabitants, all the words of the book which the king of Judah has read" (II Kings 22:16). The king then entered into a solemn covenant with the people to obey the Book of the Law and carried out by far the most thoroughgoing reform in the history of the kingdom.

We are not concerned here with the reform itself. We are concerned with the fact that the prophet who was consulted about the book was a woman, Huldah. The king gave a general command to inquire of the Lord.

He did not indicate any specific prophet to be consulted. So five men, including the chief officers of the king, set off to find Huldah. Huldah is described first of all as "the prophet,"[57] and then, according to Hebrew custom for designating women, as the wife of Shallum, a minor Temple official. We are told that Huldah lived in the Second Quarter of Jerusalem, that is, a residential area near the Temple and the king's palace. So presumably the men sought her out in her home. She prophesied in the customary manner of the prophets, and the men brought back her word to the king. That is all we know about Huldah.

We, and many commentators, are struck by the fact that the prophet was a woman. The matter at hand was an important one, and Josiah's reforms based on the book affected the lives of many people. And the person through whom the book was validated was a woman. But the writer or writers of the book of Kings were in no way struck by the fact that the men consulted a woman. The woman *was* a prophet and therefore competent to speak for God. Her sex was irrelevant.

Not many women prophets are mentioned in either the Old or the New Testament, but whenever they are mentioned, it is with the same matter-of-factness (Num. 12: 1–2; Judg. 4:4–16; Neh. 6:14; Luke 2:36). Even Paul takes it for granted that women prophesy. He is only concerned that they should have their heads covered when they do so (I Cor. 11:4–5). God could and did, and presumably does still, choose women to be prophets.

Joel 2:28–29.[58]

> And it shall come to pass afterward,
> that I will pour out my spirit on all flesh;
> your sons and your daughters shall prophesy,

> your old men shall dream dreams,
> and your young men shall see visions.
> Even upon the menservants and maidservants
> in those days, I will pour out my spirit.

In the preceding two passages we have dealt with narratives about particular women, in some ways exceptional women, women placed in unusual circumstances like the Hebrew midwives or Pharaoh's daughter, or women chosen to be prophets. In this passage we are concerned with teaching, specifically about the future. Joel prophesied probably sometime in the fourth century B.C. after the return of the people from the exile.[59] Joel spoke first of a plague of locusts and drought, as imminent signs of the Day of the Lord after which God would turn and restore the fruitfulness of the land, and finally, in this passage, of God pouring out the spirit on all flesh or, at least, on all the population of Judah.

Joel was writing at a time of increasing subordination of women to men and increasing exclusion of women from any real role in worship.[60] Women and slaves were like children in that they had a master, a free man, over them. They could relate to God only indirectly, through their masters. Yet in this prophecy Joel indicated that this is not the way things will be. Women and slaves along with men—old men and young warriors—will receive the outpouring of God's Spirit. God's graciousness in the new creation is emphasized by the inclusion of women and slaves. *Even they* will receive the gift of the Spirit directly from God.

Here in the Old Testament poetic symmetry of Joel we find hints of a future in which women will be equal with men before God in receiving the outpouring of

God's Spirit. In the book of The Acts, Joel's prophecy of the outpouring of the Spirit is seen as having been fulfilled on the Day of Pentecost. Peter addresses the crowd gathered in Jerusalem for the feast and explains that Jesus' disciples who are filled with the Spirit are not drunk, "but this is what was spoken by the prophet Joel: 'And in the last days it shall be, God declares, that I will pour out my Spirit upon all flesh, and your sons and your daughters shall prophesy'" (Acts 2:16–17). The last days, or the beginning of the new creation, are in some sense here now.

II. *Stories and Teachings from the New Testament*

Mark 7:24–30; Matt. 15:21–28. In this section we will turn our attention to a New Testament passage. Most of us are familiar with the story of the healing of the Syrophoenician woman's daughter (Mark 7:24–30): Jesus had gone to Tyre, to Gentile country, and was trying to keep his presence there a secret. But immediately a Gentile woman came to him and begged him to free her daughter from a demon. Jesus said to her, "Let the children first be fully fed, for it is not right to take the children's bread and throw it to the dogs." But she answered him, "Master, even the dogs under the table eat the children's crumbs." Then Jesus said, "For this word, go; the demon has left your daughter."[61] And the child was indeed healed.

Most of us have heard sermons on this passage. We are told correctly that the children refer to the Jews and the dogs to the Gentiles. We are told that the point of the story is that Jesus' earthly ministry was to the Jews, but it did expand, or lay the basis for expansion, to include Gentiles.

But commentators and preachers alike often talk about the role of the woman in the story. They do so for good reason, although they do not often make it explicit. The story is a very unusual one: It is the woman who had the last word, not Jesus. Normally in the Gospel tradition someone (disciple, friend, enemy) presents Jesus with a statement or question, and Jesus comes back with a snappy answer. Here the pattern is reversed. So people have set out to explain or explain away why the woman should have had the last word, and why Jesus changed his mind and heeded the woman's request.

Many have argued that it was due to the woman's faith. Certainly faith is often an element in miracle stories. The paralytic is healed when Jesus sees the faith of the men in getting the paralytic through the roof to Jesus (Mark 2:3–5). When the father of the epileptic boy asks Jesus to heal the boy if possible, Jesus replies, "All things are possible to him who believes" (Mark 9:23). The father answers, "I believe; help my unbelief!" (v. 4). Matthew, elaborating on our story, rewrites it so that it is the woman's faith that leads Jesus to heal the daughter: "O woman, great is your faith! Be it done for you as you desire" (Matt. 15:28). But the element of faith is not present in the story as Mark tells it.

Others see Jesus healing the daughter because of the woman's humility as well as her faith. It is difficult to see how that can be read into the story except on the basis of preconceived notions about Jesus and the role of women. When I behave in a similar fashion—seeking out a man who is trying to keep himself hidden and demanding a personal favor from him, and that man tells me, "No, you are not eligible for it," if I answer back, "You are only seeing a part of the picture, here is the rest"—I am likely to be labeled aggressive, if not something worse. If I were properly humble, I would have said, "Sorry to bother you," and gone meekly away.

Other commentators include the woman's perseverance among the reasons why Jesus healed the daughter. Well, the woman did find him when he was trying to hide. She argued back and did not go meekly away. But in two instances of Jesus' teaching the value of perseverance—the story of the man who at midnight gets bread from his friend (Luke 11:5–8) and the story of the widow who gets justice from the unjust judge (Luke 18:1–8)—the person requesting the favor got what he or she wanted, not because the other person wished to grant it, but because that person wished to get rid of him or her. That factor does not seem to be operating in the story in Mark.

A few commentators actually acknowledge the woman's wit. Her answer is indeed a good retort. But even this is often used to demonstrate that Jesus had a sense of humor or could appreciate one. It is nice to know that Jesus did have a sense of humor, but this reason, along with the others given above, essentially ignores the dynamic of the story as it is told in the Gospel of Mark.

Jesus says, "No"; the woman replies, "But . . ." and Jesus says, "Because of (or for the sake of) this *word,* go; the demon has left your daughter." "Word" is frequently used in Mark in an absolute sense meaning "gospel" or "teachings of Jesus." But it is also often used in the sense we have here, meaning "saying," or "what has been said." In this use, "word" always refers to the *content* of the saying, not to the manner of saying. So it was what the woman said to Jesus that got him to change his mind—not why or how she said it. The point is that the woman was right—the dogs at least got the crumbs. And as a result of arguing back and being correct, the woman got what she wanted: her daughter was cured.

The story, looked at in this way, seems to have two implications for us. First, as a model, the woman by aggressive use of her intellect got what she wanted. And this is the only instance in all the canonical stories about Jesus where anyone gets Jesus to change his mind about what to do. Others, including demons, get Jesus to do things, but never to change his mind. And the person who did this was a woman. Second, we are warned not to be blinded by our own inherited conditioning into interpreting Bible passages in a manner denigrating to women. Many passages in the Bible are indeed sexist, but this one is not. And if we read the Bible with fresh eyes, we will find other passages that are not.

The point of the story itself remains that Jesus' earthly mission was to the Jews, although the basis of expansion to a Gentile mission was there. The point of the story could have been made by a man, or a child, or Jesus himself could have added the comment about crumbs. But the fact remains that the point *was* made by the woman.

Mark 3:31–35; Matt. 12:46–50; Luke 8:19–21. We retold the preceding story from the point of view of the woman involved. We could as easily have retold it emphasizing the point that Jesus did not treat women as inferior or unclean beings. The statement about dogs refers to the fact that the woman is a Gentile, not to the fact that she is a female. There are many other stories in the Gospel tradition that show Jesus' lack of discrimination against women: for example, the healings of both men and women (e.g., Luke 7:2–12; 13:10–16; 14:2–6); the statement that, in the end, women will be saved (or left behind) equally with men (Matt. 24:40–41); the story of Jesus and the Samaritan women in the Gospel of John (John 4:4–42); and perhaps most striking, the story in the Gospel of Luke in which Jesus permits a prostitute to anoint him, and compares her behavior favorably with that of his host, a righteous Pharisee (Luke 7:36–50). But rather than retell another story about Jesus, let us look at an example of his teaching:

And his mother and his brothers came, and standing outside, they sent to him, calling for him. And a crowd was seated around him, and they said to him, "Here are your mother and your brothers outside;[62] they are looking for you." And he answered them, "Who are my mother and my brothers?" And looking around at the ones sitting all around him, he said, "Here are my mother and my brothers. For whoever does the will of God, this one is my brother and my sister and my mother."[63]

The point of the teaching is evident: the true kindred of Jesus are those who associate with Jesus, who do the will of God, not those who are related to him by blood ties. Commentators generally agree on this. The same point is made in Luke 11:27–28.

A woman in the crowd raised her voice and said to him, "Blessed is the womb that bore you, and the breasts that you sucked!" But he said, "Blessed rather are those who hear the word of God and keep it!"

Commentators, however, generally overlook the radicalism of this teaching in two respects: first, Jesus' treatment of his mother, and second, Jesus' inclusion of mothers and sisters among his true relations. In both of these instances, Jesus is making a radical break with his culture and religion.

It would seem to be merely common courtesy for Jesus to go out and speak to his mother when she is asking for him. But more than that, it would be his religious duty. The directive to honor your father and mother is one of the Ten Commandments (Ex. 20:12; Deut. 5:16). Further, Jesus in the Gospel of Mark twice refers to it with approval as a commandment of God (Mark 7:9–13; 10:19). Yet in this instance he ignores his blood mother and calls the women who are presumably among the crowd sitting around him his "mother." There is something more important than the parental relationship.

Secondly, in defining his true relatives as those who do the will of God, Jesus includes "sister" and "mother" — that is, women—equally with "brother" men. In the Judaism of the time, women were thought to be decidedly inferior to men. Like non-Jewish slaves and children (minors), they had a master over them (father or husband), and so were not equal with men before God.[64] As for doing the will of God, a woman was not even permitted to learn it. Because she was female, she was exempt from the requirement to learn the Torah, the written will of God. Furthermore, it would have been virtually impossible for a woman to do so. The schools attached to the synagogues were open only to men and boys. A woman studying the Law was a very rare exception. One rabbi writing about A.D. 90 said, "If a man gives his daughter a knowledge of the Law it is as though he taught her lechery," and "Better to burn the Torah than to teach it to women."[65] Jesus' behavior is in stark contrast. Not only does he openly teach women along with men (see Luke 10:38–42), and have women followers (Luke 8:1–3; Mark 15:41), but he takes it for granted that women, equally with men, can do the will of God, and thereby be his true kindred.

The passage in Mark, ch. 3, and its parallels in Matthew and Luke, then, represent a radical redefinition of the Old Testament and Jewish relationship between women and men and God. In order to see this we have had to look not only at the Biblical text but also at the religious and social norms of Jesus' time. In the Old Testament law, the only area in which a woman is regarded as the equal of a man, and accorded equal honor, is in her role as mother or parent.[66] In Jesus' teaching, the biological role of mother does not in itself give a woman status or honor. What is important for any woman, as for any man, is to do the will of God, and in so doing, she, like her brother, is a true relative of Jesus.

Galatians 3:27–28.
For as many of you as were baptized into Christ have put on Christ. There is neither Jew nor Greek, there is neither slave nor free, there is neither male nor female; for you are all one in Christ Jesus.

The apostle Paul made various statements about the role of women in church and their place in the order of creation (see especially I Cor., chs. 11 and 14), which along with some passages in the later letters have been used and still are being used to justify the inferior position of women in society and in the church. But Paul, in the passage quoted above, has also provided a basic theological statement of the equality of women and men.

The statement itself is straightforward and absolute enough. For those who are baptized—that is, those in the church—the old grounds for discrimination and oppression, which have found their justification in the Old Testament law and in the culture of Paul's time, are no longer valid. The Jew is not superior to the Greek (the heathen or the Gentile). The free man is no longer superior to the slave. (Today we might say the white person to the black person, or the First World to the Third World.) And man is no longer superior to woman. "The coming of Christ rules out the need for religious, economic and sexually designated subordinating roles."[67] And since these divisions are broken through and overcome in baptism, discrimination based on them is ruled out now, not just in some future new age of freedom. "Therefore, if anyone is in Christ, he or she is a new creation" (II Cor. 5:17).[68]

If the interpretation of Paul's theological proclamation in Gal. 3:27–28 is as clear-cut as we have described, and it is, how can scholars and preachers and many churchmen continue to cite the Biblical authority of Paul to justify the inferior position of women in society and in the church? In part, of course, the answer lies in the human, in this case male, tendency to emphasize material that supports its own biases and to "overlook" or ignore contrary material.

But the answer also lies in the way commentators have "harmonized" the various statements of Paul concerning women.[69] The method has been to make a distinction between the realms in which Paul's statements are to apply. The theological statement of equality that we have been studying applies only to the matter of individual salvation. The gift of grace is available to women, as well as to men, without distinction. However, other statements, such as "he [man] is the image and glory of God; but woman is the glory of man" (I Cor.

11:7), which argue that the subordination of women to men is part of God's order of creation are taken as normative—and God's will—for the conduct of society and of the church.

Even this interpretation is an improvement over the typical view of women in the Judaism of Paul's time. At least women are equal "before God," if not before men. The absurdity of this division in realms of application, however, can be seen if we look for a moment at the second of the three dichotomies of Paul—slave vs. free. The Biblical situation is very similar to that of male vs. female. The Old and New Testaments, on the whole, reflect the culture of the times in which they were written and assume the subordinate position of slaves and women. Paul's own statements about slavery reflect the same range that they do about women: here in the Galatians passage, wiping out the inferiority of slaves; and elsewhere, appearing to take the institution of slavery for granted (I Cor. 7:17–24; Philemon).

Many Christians through the centuries have maintained the same division in applying these texts. Slaves certainly could be saved by God. Many plantation owners in the South built chapels for their slaves. But in everyday life slaves should be obedient to their masters —this was the will of God. Today it would be difficult to find anyone who would be willing to justify slavery— the outright ownership of persons—as part of the proper ordering of society according to God's will. We have come to view slavery as evil—if not yet all forms of economic oppression. And in turning to the Bible, we note that many of the Old Testament laws concerning slaves were attempts to protect them from undue abuse; we accept Paul's theological formulation in Galatians as authoritative; and we rejoice that we have

moved that much nearer to a just society and the new
creation in the abolition of slavery. In this instance, we
take it for granted that what is true before God should
also be made real in society. We see no need to perpetu-
ate earlier social conditions reflected in Biblical literature. Do we not pray "Thy will be done on earth as it
is in heaven"?

Nor can it be argued that Paul thought of his statement concerning Gentiles, women, and slaves as applying only in the realm of individual salvation, and not in
the life of the church. Paul, in all his letters except
Romans, was reacting to specific situations or problems
in his churches. And in the letter to the Galatian
churches Paul was responding precisely to a practical
problem of the relationship between Jew and Gentile in
those churches. Evidently the people in the churches
that Paul started in Galatia were Greeks. Now Paul had
heard that some people in those churches, or missionaries to them, were trying to persuade these new Christians to be circumcised—that is, to become first a Jew
in order that they might become Christian. Paul was
horrified (Gal. 1:6–9). If the Galatian Christians accepted circumcision, he saw them as severing themselves from freedom and grace in Christ and placing
themselves in bondage to the old law (Gal. 3:2; 4:21;
5:1–5). Paul devoted much of this letter to an argument
that the Old Testament law was a stage in the development of salvation history, which has now been super-
seded by the revelation of God in Christ, as was promised in the Old Testament. That is, Paul presented a
formal justification for his statement that there was no
longer any distinction or discrimination between Jew
and Greek, and clearly intended this equality to be the
everyday reality in the churches. "For in Christ Jesus

neither circumcision nor uncircumsion is of any avail, but faith working through love" (Gal. 5:6).

Nowhere in the letters of Paul, nor elsewhere in the New Testament, is there any extended theological argument for the overcoming of the discrimination between slave and free or female and male. But then these were not major issues in the New Testament period, whereas the very possibility of including Gentiles in the Christian church and the proper relationship between Jews and Greeks within the churches were major issues and a cause of considerable conflict in early Christianity (see Acts 10:1 to 11:18; 15:1–29; Gal. 2:1–6). And the overt conflict was fully resolved during the period reflected in the New Testament writings: Greeks and Jews were equal not only before God but also in the churches.

Paul had quite enough practical problems to deal with in his churches without expending energy arguing about things that were not actual problems for him. Yet in his theological summing up of the equality of Jew and Greek in the church, he also includes the equality of slave and free, of male and female. The principle and model are there. It is our job, now that the issue of women's liberation has become a major source of conflict in society and in the churches, to work out the formal theological justification of the equality of women and men in the church, a principle lived by Jesus and formulated by Paul. And we are called to live in the present as if the new age of freedom had already arrived. And as we strive for and move toward the real equality and mutuality of women and men in the lives of the churches, we are helping to bring into actuality, however imperfectly, the life of the new age.

III. *Suggestions for Reading Biblical Passages*

1. As far as possible, try to read the Bible without preconceptions, no matter how familiar you are with any particular story. Try not to read through the eyes of two thousand years of Christian *and* androcentric interpretation, but read freshly and with an open mind as you would read a story or watch a movie. It is helpful to use different translations of the Bible so that you are not lulled by familiar words.

2. Whenever there is a woman or women in a Biblical passage, always reread or retell the story from the viewpoint of the woman. Imagine yourself to be that woman, and reread the story with yourself as the central character. Frequently, this is all that is necessary to give you an entirely different perspective on a passage. Some of the women may emerge as admirable people, others as not so admirable, but they will at least emerge as people, as whole human beings.[70]

3. Look for what is omitted in a text, as well as what is included. For instance, in the portrait of a good wife in Prov. 31:10–29, the wife is never described as obedient or subordinate to her husband. It is stated that "she does him good, and not harm, all the days of her life" (Prov. 31:12). But this is not necessarily best accomplished by following her husband's will rather than using her own good judgment!

4. Pay attention to the context of a passage. When we see as part of the whole exodus-liberation event the women who surrounded the birth of Moses, they become God's agents and not only part of a domestic prelude. The context of Paul's statement in Galatians about neither Jew nor Greek, male nor female, within his

overall argument, shows that Paul is not talking about the private matter of individual salvation, but about the life of the church.

5. Knowledge of social and cultural environment, particularly of the role—or non-role—of women in the times in which the Bible was written, can be very helpful in understanding and interpreting texts. Jesus' open and nondiscriminatory behavior with women is in striking contrast to the normal behavior of Jewish men toward women.[71] Only by knowing the background can we discriminate between material that reflects the culture of its times and material that contrasts with it.

6. Standard commentaries should be used with discretion and compared with interpretations such as those provided in the Notes and Additional Resources in this book. They are convenient and useful compendiums of background information and interpretation. Since we no longer live in the same worlds in which the writers of the Bible did, we need commentaries to help us in our reading. But we should look at a variety of interpretations, because sometimes explanations of a text are either reading into a passage or explaining away a passage. All interpretations should also be checked against the passage itself, to see if they appear to reflect the text and its context.

4

CHANGING LANGUAGE
AND THE CHURCH

Letty M. Russell

Living language changes as a reflection of changing human experience and consciousness. For this reason we must be concerned with whether the language we use is an authentic expression of that human experience. As we proceed with Biblical interpretation, it is important to change the language in a way that is faithful to our growing knowledge of the original texts and languages as well as to the need for conveying the insights of the original story in ever-new cultural and linguistic contexts.[72]

Changes in language constantly interact with our faith and actions in Christian communities. New insights into interpretation arise out of these communities as Christians seek to participate in the story of God's actions or mission in the world. Our churches are also changing and need to be changed and reformed. As they work to become genuinely inclusive of all sexes, races, classes, and cultures, their life-styles and organizational structures must be altered so that the ministry of the whole people of God is recognized and encouraged. At the same time, new experiences of inclusive community and organization lead to newly inclusive language in worship, study, and daily life.

In examining this question of changing language, it is important that we begin with a story of the way interpretation and language changed as a result of the resurrection. Then we can turn to look at some of the implications this has for people who are attempting to use inclusive language in the church and theology today. This gives us at least a few clues about ways we can move ahead in interpreting the living faith in Jesus Christ that shapes our lives.

I. *Resurrection Hermeneutics*

THE LIBERATING WORD is a guide to resurrection hermeneutics. As we have learned, the Greek-based word used to describe the process of translation, explanation, or interpretation is "hermeneutics." This word appears in the New Testament in Luke's story of how Christ began the process of interpreting the Old Testament in the light of resurrection, on the road to Emmaus (Luke 24:13–35). It also appears in I Corinthians as Paul points out that the Spirit of Christ continues to grant gifts of interpretation in the church (I Cor. 12: 10,30; 14:5,13,27).

"And their eyes were opened. . . ." Luke 24:13–35 describes a dialogue in which the risen Christ not only interprets the Scriptures so that the disciples may understand the meaning of his life, death, and resurrection, but also acts out his word so that their eyes are opened to see what he has been saying (v. 31). This account has significant clues for the ways in which the story of God's actions comes alive in the hearts and actions of Christ's followers.[73] The interpretation takes

place *along the road*—in the midst of daily actions, not just in worship or in scholars' studies. It also happens in the context of *human community*—as Jesus and the disciples are talking and discussing together. Christ speaks to us in and through our willingness to wrestle together with the texts. The climax of the story is a *self-revealing event* in which Christ makes himself known in the breaking of bread so that the disciples receive "eyes of faith" to see the reality of their living Lord. The result is an *act of witness* as the disciples run to share the good news with others.

"He interpreted to them in all the scriptures. . . . " This is what resurrection hermeneutics is all about: meeting God in Jesus Christ through daily actions and discussion together so that our hearts, minds, actions—and even our language—are changed (v. 27). Because of the resurrection, the followers of Jesus Christ were constrained to continue the story of God's action, interpreting the meaning of the Old Testament in the New Testament in the light of its fulfillment, ascribing titles of divine honor to Jesus and pointing to the expectation of God's continuing action in opening the future and hope to all humanity.

These same factors are present today as we seek to do Biblical interpretation in the light of a new change of consciousness. What does it mean to struggle with the words of Gal. 3:28 in the way that Paul struggled with the issue of breaking barriers between "Jew and Greek," and, more recently, that people have struggled with breaking barriers between "slave and free"? In our time, the realization that "the most primary division of God's creation is overcome—that between "male and female"—leads us back to interpreting what

Scriptures mean for this aspect of our life in Christ.[74] The interpretation itself takes on meaning only as we are willing to journey on the road to new inclusiveness in community with others. The center of our interpretive process remains the self-revealing event in which Christ made it known, not only in his earthly dealings with women but also in his resurrection appearances to women, that men and women are equally welcome as witnesses and full participants in the new age.[75] Our witness involves the scandal of living out this insight into the meaning of God's actions in our churches and lives, whether or not this full partnership is a fact in the society around us.

II. *Changing Language and the Church*

Many churches are beginning to make changes in language as they attempt to implement the gospel mandate of full equality for all human beings. These changes reflect political actions of women and men who are no longer willing to see women excluded by the traditional male language of constitutions, liturgies, hymns, and Biblical interpretations. But they also reflect a struggle to bring our political actions into line with recent theological insights into the meaning of the gospel message in relation to women. Task forces report to their national bodies, bringing strong recommendations for change.[76] Other study groups are appointed to address themselves to eliminating the so-called "generic" masculine nouns and pronouns in worship, constitutions, and other official church documents.[77] Almost every denomination and ecumenical organization has groups organized around issues related to the community of women and men in church and society, and most of these send out regular newsletters and communications.

Although these groups are working on many issues, all of them reflect the growing consensus that the English usage of such words as "man," "men," "his," "mankind," "brotherhood" in the *generic sense* seems to reflect conscious or unconscious sexist structures and attitudes in church and society. Everyone is included by these words, but only in the sense that man is the norm for human and woman is simply a less-than-human appendage of man. It is *generic nonsense* to say that women are included linguistically by such male terms when they are excluded both socially and linguistically from the male-oriented conduct of worship, styles of government, and religious life.

In adjusting language in reference to persons, the churches have been aided by the recent publication of various guidelines for nonsexist language.[78] These guidelines attempt to help writers and speakers in respect to eliminating sexist and racist attitudes from their portrayals of human beings. They urge the overcoming of stereotyped or demeaning descriptions of all groups as well as the elimination of the generic usage of male terms.

A few of the suggestions made are the following:

1. Substituting such terms as "humanity," "humankind," "human beings," "humans," "persons," "people," "everyone," "folk" for "man," etc., in the generic sense.

2. Avoiding masculine pronouns to refer to men and women together by using "he and she," "hers and his," or by shifting to the plural form.

3. Avoiding use of male-dominant phrases where all the people of God are to be included. Such shifts as the

following are helpful: "sons of God" to "children of God"; "faith of our fathers" to "faith of our forebears, ancestors, or forerunners"; "pray, brethren" to "pray, brothers and sisters." "Fellowship" is a translation of the Greek *koinonia,* which also may be rendered as "participation," "communion," "community," or "partnership."

4. Calling both women and men by their full names; both by first or last names; both by titles. For instance: "John Brown and his wife" becomes "John and Sally Brown," or "John Brown and Sally Smith" if she uses her own last name. Titles and use of first or last name are made uniform in lists of people. Where possible, the term of address is that which a person prefers: Mr., Ms., Miss, Mrs., Dr., Rev., etc.; or no titles are used.

5. Alternating references to women and men in speech and writing. "Men and women" should alternate with "women and men," "hers and his" with "his and hers," and illustrations and role references should be mixed and not stereotyped.

6. Using inclusive terminology for generic or occupational groupings. For instance: "salesperson," not "salesman"; "clergy, clergy persons, clergy women and men," not "clergymen"; "laity, lay men and women," not "laymen"; "clergy and spouses," not "clergy and wives"; "chairperson, moderator, convener," not "chairman"; "minister, poet, author, priest," not words for women ending in -ess.

One of the pronouns to be avoided in language about people and the church is "she." A collectivity is normally neuter in English, not feminine. In addition to this, the regular use of feminine metaphors and pronouns for the church tends to reflect a cultural stereotype that the feminine is inferior to the masculine, as in the metaphor of a feminine church and a masculine God. It reflects a setting in which God and husband were identified as Lord, and Israel, church, and wife were identified as servant. When the feminine term is used for the church, it appears to leave men out in their role as part of the servant people. In addition, it often creates a false superiority among male clergy, who think of themselves as representing Christ, whereas they are simply a part of the whole people of God, who are all Christ's representatives. In Eph. 5:21–32 such a metaphor uses the relationship of husband and wife to describe the mystery of Christ and the church. The key to this metaphor is the mystery of the closeness of mutual relationship. But our assumptions often prevent us from seeing that *both sides* of the relationship involve sacrifice and service. Men and women love and serve God because God has chosen in Christ to be present with them in suffering service. Our struggle with changing language reflects a commitment as men and women alike to continue this love and service in ways that contribute to wholeness and mutuality in community.

III. *Changing Language and Theology*

Theology as practiced in seminaries and pulpits has long been almost exclusively a male domain. It is not surprising, therefore, that conscious and unconscious sexism is reflected in the values, interpretation, and formulation of the Christian faith. Yet theology, by its very nature, is constantly changing. It is the way in which we think (-logy) about God (theo-), as God is revealed in and through the Word in the world. As the world changes, theological styles change and Christians strive to express the meaning of the gospel in ways that it can be heard and understood as good news of deliverance. So far, this continuing dialogue, with eyes of faith reflecting on Scripture, tradition, and experience, has seldom included the participation of women and other oppressed groups. However, there is hope! The Spirit of Christ inspires us anew in each generation. As the "outsiders" begin to articulate their experience of faith in congregations, seminaries, and pulpits, it is likely that professional theologians (women and men) will begin to struggle with what this means for all dimensions of our faith.

This process of interpretation, based on more inclusive use of the ways women and men experience the Christ event, is already beginning.[79] Not only are women in all walks of life participating together in the reformulation of theological perspectives but also men and women are gradually beginning to study the many aspects related to interpretation and language. Theological working groups are active in denominations and ecumenical organizations, trying to seek out the implications of the shifting consciousness of women and men for the interpretation of the Christian faith. For instance, the United Presbyterians have just concluded the first phase of a study on "Language About God"; the Lutheran Church in America is working on the concern for inclusive language; and the World Council of Churches has begun an international study on "The Community of Women and Men in the Church."[80]

Adjusting our language, symbols, and concepts in reference to God is difficult and dangerous. These references are rooted in Biblical language and in the language of theological traditions over the centuries. Changes that are "easy" to make so they are in line with current ideologies of human liberation may not necessarily be a faithful expression of the whole gospel message. If they too easily resolve the tensions inherent in all metaphors for the mystery of God, they may lose hard-won ecumenical insights of the past or create changes that may become binding or distorting for future generations of Christians. Nevertheless, changed perceptions of reality are bound to present the challenge for needed reinterpretation of the images and doctrines used to interpret the continuing experience of God in Jesus Christ.[81] Much of this takes time for research, dialogue, and experiment. It also takes time for new symbols to emerge out of our collective experiences of reality, symbols that genuinely point beyond themselves to the mystery of God.[82]

The Second Commandment warns the people of God against making graven images of God (Deut. 5:8). Yet in the symbols and words of the Old Testament we find a constant tension between the idea of God as a male deity of the Hebrew people and the ever-growing conviction that God is not specified or limited by any masculinity.[83] As the monotheism of the Old Testament developed, the attributes and power of Yahweh were universalized to include many of those formerly ascribed to the female and male deities of Israel's neighbors. Along with this assertion of the holiness and exclusive nature of God as one God are heard the reminders of prophets such as Hosea and Isaiah: "I am God and not man, the Holy One in your midst" (Hos. 11:9); "I, I am the Lord, besides me there is no Savior. I declared and saved and proclaimed, when there was no strange God among you; and you are my witnesses" (Isa. 43:11–12).[84]

Despite the assertion of God's transcendence of any human image, male or female, it was to be expected that in a patriarchal culture, ruled by men, the proper titles of respect for God would normally make use of masculine terms. This did not exclude the use of feminine imagery, but, given the inferiority of women in the culture, it was not generally within the thought pattern of that society to ascribe honor to God by using feminine images. As studies have shown, God is referred to from time to time through images generally associated with women: serving, sheltering, mothering.[85] But the primary way God was known was through self-revealing actions in relation to the story of Israel and not through lists of either masculine or feminine attributes.

Jesus himself, in contrast to the reticence of the Old Testament writers in using the term "Father" for God, in the Gospel accounts frequently speaks of God as his Father. The Father-Son imagery of the New Testement is an important theological affirmation of the oneness and unity of Christ with God and was an appropriate designation of this relationship, given the respective roles of men and women in that society. But stress can also be placed on oneness in will and mission through the metaphor of God's active Word (John 1:1–5) or through the metaphor of Jesus as the Second Humankind who through God's design transcends his concrete cultural context as male and Jew.[86]

Given our new appreciation of the fact that both male and female are created in God's image (Gen. 1:27) and that in Jesus Christ a new age has begun which has broken down the old dichotomies between male and female (Gal. 3:28), it is important to broaden our metaphors for God so that God both comprehends and transcends the fullest range of changing human experience. Guides to nonsexist language have been written, and some of these deal with language about God. (See "Additional Resources," Section III.)

Some of the suggestions in regard to language about God that are being explored are the following:

1. Names for God should avoid excessive use of male imagery and pronouns and those which model the social relationships of patriarchal culture, such as "Father," "King," "Master." God can be referred to by the Hebrew name "Yahweh" or simply by repeating the word "God" rather than using masculine pronouns. It is also helpful to include references in both masculine and feminine pairs (Mother and Father; he and she) or to describe God in metaphors that include female models such as the woman with the lost coin (Luke 15: 8–10).[87] The interchangeable use of pronouns and images is not intended to continue our stereotypes of masculine and feminine roles, but to free ourselves from these stereotypes by experiencing the mixture of these roles in metaphors for God.

2. Avoiding the use of the words "Our Father" unless they are balanced with other metaphors, both because of the patriarchal overtones of its usage and because of the changing familial structures that often make excessive use of "father" a means of excluding not only mother and women but also children who do not have a father or a loving father image. Some people use the words "Our Parent" or "Our God" in the Lord's Prayer, but this does not have the close symbolic overtones of Jesus' words (Matt. 6:9–13; Luke 11:2–4). Another possibility in relation to this prayer would be to use the early liturgical words reflecting Jesus' own use of Aramaic, "*Abba,* Father" (Mark 14:36; Rom. 8:15; Gal. 4:6). To pray using the word *Abba* has the advantage of pointing to Jesus' use of the intimate form of address as an expression of his closeness to God. Then the words em-

phasize that we pray as Jesus and the Spirit teach us to pray by relating to God in love, gratitude, and obedience, not because of the present meaning of the word "Father." In attempting to relate our prayers to the contemporary situation and to Jesus' use of the familiar term *Abba,* we can also employ the second person pronoun "you" rather than the archaic form "thee."

3. Emphasizing nonsex specific words for God, such as Spirit, Wisdom, Glory, Holy One, Eternal One, Rock, Fire, First and Last, Sustainer, Liberator, Creator, Advocate, Maker, Defender, Friend, Nurturer.

4. Speaking about Jesus as male only when the designation refers to his earthly life as a male (*anēr* in Greek or *ʾīsh* in Hebrew), and using the word "humankind" or "person" (*anthrōpos* in Greek or *ʾādām* in Hebrew) when describing his role in representing new humanity as Liberator, Redeemer, and Savior. We can recognize that male pronouns for Jesus emphasize the scandal of the particularity of his incarnation as a male Jew of the first century. Also, we might use the word "Lord" only when emphasizing the role of the risen Christ as one with God, as symbolized in its early liturgical usage (I Cor. 12:3; Eph. 4:5; Rev. 19:16). According to Phil. 2:5–11, Jesus received the divine title "Lord" because he gave his life as a servant for others.

5. Speaking of the Holy Spirit as "she" or "it." The Hebrew word *rūach* ("wind," "breath," "spirit") is usually feminine and the Greek word *pneuma* ("spirit") is neuter, but there is a tendency to use the masculine pronoun in English. Although linguistic gender is not directly related to sex and does not convey that God is actually male or female, use of the feminine pronoun may be a way of expressing the metaphorical inclusion of all human relationships in our experience of the God-

head. This raises people's consciousness about the problem of metaphors that are perceived by some as exclusive of women.[88] The use of feminine as well as masculine metaphors for God occurs in church traditions,
especially among the mystics and in some Eastern
churches where the Holy Spirit is sometimes referred
to in feminine terms or images.[89]

In all these attempts to balance the metaphors for the
Trinity it should be remembered that, in theological
tradition, there is an equality of partnership among the
three members and, though there is distinction in their
missions, there is no separation. The whole Trinity, as
one, both includes and transcends all the masculine and
feminine metaphors we might use. When we describe
the Trinity, it is not sufficient just to add words with
traditional feminine overtones. The words used should
also be an expression of the nature of God as experienced in the Christian community. In addition to
recognizing the power of language, symbols, and metaphors to affect not only our views of God but also our
views of ourselves, we must be constantly aware that
the mystery of God is beyond all our attempts at naming or creating idols and images, whether old or new
(Ex. 3:13–15).

IV. *Interpreting the Bible in New Contexts*

We are still on the road with others, guided by the
self-revelation of Christ's Spirit in our lives. This road is
leading us to search for new ways of interpreting the
Bible that express the changing context of our journey
of faith. In this strange and bewildering journey into
questions of language and interpretation there are, per-

haps, a few clues that can help us to make our way together.

1. *New actions lead to new language,* insights, and imagery. We will not be able to have our eyes opened to understand the Scriptures with new vision unless we are "on the road." It takes practice in daily life, worship, and actions to overcome our sexist angles of vision and our language customs, whether we be male or female. No amount of years of study or tools of exegesis can be of much help unless we have committed ourselves to act out the words of Gal. 3:28 and opened ourselves to the leading of the Holy Spirit in discovering what this will mean for ourselves and our sisters and brothers in Jesus Christ.

2. *Every Christian is a theologian,* and the whole church must be engaged in the theological task of thinking about God as God is known in and through the Word in the world. Only by the action and reflection of the whole people of God will the full possibility of insights into the meaning of the gospel be shared and lived. We all need the help of scholarly research and the tools of interpretation. Yet no amount of learning will help faith to shape life if it is not lived out in hope and love. Professional theologians, like other human beings, have biases and limitations. Only as all Christians join the task of interpretation, and take it seriously as a question of their own identity and maturity of faith, will the difficult task of liberating the Word go forward.

3. *Translation is a continuing process.* As Phyllis Trible puts it: "Since no exegesis is exempt from the experience of the exegete, no interpretation is fixed once and for all. Clearly the hermeneutical task requires un-

derstanding the Bible as dynamic literature engaged
with continuing experience."[90] It is up to women and
men who are concerned with nonsexist interpretation
to reread and discover the lost dimensions of the Bible
and to seek out new angles of vision. In such work of
reading and translation it is important to return to the
original languages by means of interlinear translations,
dictionaries, and word books if we are not familiar with
Hebrew and Greek.

Some of the changes we might seek to make may be
in the original text, but have been obscured by linguistic patterns or sexist bias in the translations. For instance, the King James Version of 1611 translated II
Cor. 5:17: "Therefore if any man be in Christ, he is a
new creature." The Revised Standard Version renders
this: "Therefore, if any one is in Christ, he is a new
creation," yet the Greek original uses neither the word
"man" nor a masculine pronoun. The Revision Committee of *The Worshipbook* has suggested the following
translation: "Anyone in Christ is of the New Creation."[91] Another small example is to be seen in the RSV
translation of Gen. 3:6, in which Adam's presence with
Eve in the discussion with the snake is obscured: "She
gave some to her husband, and he ate." The Hebrew
says, "She gave some to her husband *with her,* and he
ate."[92]

There are other changes in translation that we may
want to make in a particular setting of worship or study
that are faithful to the message and yet more clearly
inclusive for the people involved. In public readings of
the Bible, however, it is important to check the passage
beforehand and to make clear what translation or para-
phrase is being used.

4. *Christian community is a continuing process.* It is

the presence of Christ in and through the Word, Sacraments, and persons that helps us to discern the working of the Spirit (I Cor. 12:10). This process of discernment can help us take a prophetic stance over against society when necessary, yet at the same time seek to understand the signs of the times as we participate in God's actions of justice and love. The reason for changing the church is not just that society changes. It is for the sake of continued renewal of the ways we express the mission and message of Jesus Christ. A congregation that is not alive and changing may be living on frozen assets and debits of the past. Community is created as a gift of life by Christ, and its continuing possibility is dependent on our commitment to continue the dialogue with Christ in a supportive and caring way with others.

The liberating Word is the power of the gospel to renew our lives continually, opening them to freedom and future. It is important to guard the power of that original story against distortion and not to write into it our own limited perspectives. In this way we retain the witness to God's action in the history of Israel, Jesus Christ, and the church. It is possible for us to be faithful to the Biblical message while seeking out the most accurate version of that story and then trying to help it to speak clearly in today's world. The many parts of the Bible that are embedded in patriarchal contexts out of which they were written can be seen clearly as such. They will also be seen by coming generations if we work to make these texts clear. It is not necessary to rewrite or add to the Bible, although new translations by scholars are always needed. We would then add our limited and much more distant versions to the earliest witness of God's liberating actions. The Bible is a witness to the

promise that God continues to be with us as Creator,
Liberator, and Advocate in every generation. It is a
story that continues, in any case, as we enter into that
story, following Christ along the road toward the future.

Our focus on a nonsexist interpretation of the Bible
should assist in liberating the Word so it can be heard
in the language and perspectives of women and other
oppressed groups today. It is a way of participating in
God's continuing concern for downtrodden and marginal people. This difficult and critical process of interpretation can have an over-plus value for anyone who
takes it seriously. The questions raised about our own
self-identity and calling as Christians make it clear to us
that we cannot leave it only to others to decide the
answers for us. Newly involved with what the liberating
Word means for us, we will want to seek out the best
tools possible for expressing its message. In the end, this
wrestling with the texts and with ourselves may open
our eyes more clearly to the gospel message so that our
"hearts burn within us" (Luke 24:32) as we continue
that Emmaus dialogue along the road.

SUGGESTIONS
FOR STUDY AND ACTION

I. *Groups Using This Guide*

The Guide was planned, written, and edited by a group and has many marks of an unfinished product. This is intentional, because the GUIDE is not a finished piece of research but an invitation to others to join together in the discussion. The writers have worked together with others to include the readers in an ongoing discussion of Biblical interpretation in a feminist perspective. They invite others to work together in the context of their own interpretive journey. Although it is also a resource for individual use, the Guide presents complex and provisional material that is well suited for discussion and collective research and reflection.

A variety of groups may find the Guide helpful in their study and action:

Task forces or committees on worship, education, language, or church organization might use it as background for the study of feminist issues related to decisions about changing liturgical, educational, or organizational forms at a local, regional, or national level.

Bible study groups might select the passages from one or all of the chapters for study, using the Guide and supplementary materials as they take a new look at the texts. Additional passages selected by the group might expand the discussion, with the suggestions in this book being used as a tool for study.

Theological students who are interested in feminist or liberation theology could utilize the Guide as one collective expression of feminists who view the Biblical tradition as a key factor in understanding or misunderstanding the liberating actions of God.

Preachers and other persons who prepare sermons or church publications could reflect together on ways of using the Guide in order to make the spoken and the written word more inclusive of the changing experience of women and men.

II. *Guidelines for Group Study*

Groups studying together could discuss the Guide one chapter at a time, or choose the texts used as examples as the basis of study. Because the examples are by no means exhaustive, most groups will probably want to use the "Additional Resources" section to expand their study of passages that reflect patriarchal cultural assumptions or those which appear to contradict them.

The study should be done in *small groups* of about ten to fifteen people, meeting over a period of weeks or intensively for one week or a weekend. The groups can be inclusively of men and women or be designed for separate groups. If the group is all of one sex, it is always interesting to share questions and insights with groups of the other sex. The makeup of the group should contain as wide a variety of experiences, races, ages, and points of view as possible. In this way it will provide an opportunity to *risk* the process of changing ideas that comes through frank and open confrontation and discussion among people of different walks of life.

There should be *no one teacher or speaker* for a study group. A moderator, convener, or resource person would be responsible for helping the entire group participate in the discussion. If possible, the moderator should be an experienced group leader. As the group begins to probe the meaning of Biblical texts, it would need to make sure that some persons in it have consulted other resources and commentaries. It may wish to invite a Biblical scholar to visit as a resource for clarification of a particular aspect of its study. But accepting the opinion of experts is no substitute for persons' trying to raise their own questions and understand for themselves the variety of ways in which a passage might be interpreted.

In advance, all participants should *study the text* of the Guide or of the Biblical passage selected and think about what they have discovered. A helpful aid in this may be some of the "Questions and Suggestions for Study and Action" listed below. During the discussion itself the questions and observations should come from the entire group. A good way to give everyone an opportunity to participate is to go around the group and collect the questions or topics before beginning to discuss them one at a time.

Remember that this Guide is a *starter for thought and action.* If the questions raised are not your own, work out your own formulation of questions for discussion. If the material seems too theological or too vague, look to your group members to make it concrete, personal, and social. Remember that often such discussion of changing points of view appears to be "nonsense" until we experience these views in our own actions or hear the testimony of others. If the book provokes you to violent disagreement, just go ahead and figure out where you stand and why. The writers do not pretend that there is only one answer to the topics or interpretations under discussion. Remember, also, that in the actual discussion the group is the most important resource as it reflects on the Biblical materials and interpretations in the light of its own collective experience.

III. *Questions and Suggestions for Study and Action*

The following suggestions and questions for each chapter can be used by individuals and groups in their endeavor to search out their own forms of nonsexist interpretation.

Introduction: *The Liberating Word*

1. In what sense do you perceive this Guide as "long overdue" and yet "premature"?
2. How would you explain the way the Word of God liberates or does not liberate us? Give examples of ways this has happened in your life.
3. Give examples of the ways in which language is used to reinforce discrimination in church and society.
4. Plan and carry out a nonsexist worship service, giving attention to Scripture readings, sermons, prayers, litanies, and hymns. Reflect on your experience after the service.
5. Go through your hymnal and mark the hymns that

are inclusive of women and men in their metaphors and language.

Chapter 1. *Biblical Authority and Interpretation*

1. How do you interpret the expression "The Bible is the Word of God"? In what ways does it speak to you and to others?
2. Describe some of the shifts of interpretation that you can discern within the Bible itself as the history of the people of God unfolds.
3. Give examples of Biblical interpretation from other ages or your own life that, in your opinion, reveal sexist bias.
4. What are the steps you usually use in working to understand a particular Biblical passage? How do they compare with "A Proposed Model for Biblical Interpretation"?
5. Select three of your favorite Biblical passages and discuss how your response to them is influenced by being a man or a woman. Would you select any different ones after reading this Guide?

Chapter 2: *Interpreting Patriarchal Traditions*

1. On what basis can a passage be said to reflect "patriarchal culture" or an interpretation be said to be "androcentric"?
2. Discuss the contrasting roles of women, men, and children in Biblical times and in your present experience.
3. How do you explain the attitude of Jesus toward

women, which ran counter to the prevailing religious and cultural views?

4. Discuss the pattern of sermons you have heard in the last year and reflect on how often they are drawn from texts that have a degrading view of women or that ignore the role of women. How did the interpretation of these passages compare with the "Suggestions for Interpreting Androcentric Texts in the Bible"?

5. If you seem to discover bias in this respect, discuss it with the preacher or the worship committee if they are not regularly present in the group.

Chapter 3. *Images of Women*

1. In what sense can a Biblical text be said to portray women in a positive light? Would the writers of the stories have the same view of this as your group?

2. How do you react to the assertion that passages which contradict patriarchal assumptions about women are closer to the Biblical motif of God's concern for the oppressed and outsiders?

3. Select your favorite Biblical passage about a woman and about a man. Reflect with one another about what you see in the roles of these people.

4. Study a story such as Gen., ch. 12, from the perspective of a woman by placing yourself in the role of the woman in the story. Act the story out through role-playing and then discuss what you discover and whether this changes your angle of vision.

5. If the Holy Spirit acts through women as well as men, why is it that some churches and people find it difficult to accept the ordination of women? Pursue this discussion by looking at the "Additional Resources,"

reading articles, and discussing actual experiences of women clergy. If your church does not have a woman pastor, arrange a series of opportunities for women to preach and share with your congregation. Investigate whether your church has ever interviewed a woman for a pastoral position.

Chapter 4. *Changing Language and the Church*

1. If linguistic usage of gender does not necessarily suggest the sex of a word, why is it that people are so upset when asked to make their language more consciously inclusive?
2. Share stories with one another about how your interpretation of the meaning of Scripture was changed by your life experience.
3. Try changing the language of a hymn or writing your own prayer, using feminine as well as masculine images of God and discuss this experience. Share the results of your work in a worship service or in some publication.
4. Make a list of feminine images of God that you have discovered from your own reading and the "Additional Resources." Discuss how you react to these as women and as men.
5. Write a set of language guidelines for use in public meetings, worship, and publications in your own church. Discuss the theological and social implications of the implementation of such guidelines.

BIOGRAPHICAL SKETCHES
OF CONTRIBUTORS

JOANNA DEWEY is a doctoral candidate in Biblical Studies at the Graduate Theological Union in Berkeley, California. She has been a teaching fellow in New Testament at the Church Divinity School of the Pacific and at Berkeley. She has recently completed a book: *Disciples of the Way: Mark on Discipleship* (Women's Division, The United Methodist Church, 1976).

ELISABETH SCHÜSSLER FIORENZA is Associate Professor of Theology at the University of Notre Dame. She has also taught New Testament studies at the University of Münster, Germany, and at Union Theological Seminary, New York. She has published books and articles on the role of women in theology and church and on various New Testament questions. She is associate editor of the *Journal of Biblical Literature, The Catholic Biblical Quarterly, Horizons,* and *Cross Currents.* She is a member of the Task Force of the Ad Hoc Committee on Women in Society and the Church of the National Council of Catholic Bishops and a consultant to the Task Force on Women in Church and Society of the Catholic Theological Society of America.

EMILY V. GIBBES, as Associate General Secretary for Education and Ministry of the National Council of Churches, is the Executive of the Division of Education and Ministry (formerly the Division of Christian Education of the NCC). In this capacity she coordinated the work of the Task Force on Sexism and the Bible.

SHARON H. RINGE is a doctoral candidate and tutor in New Testament at Union Theological Seminary in New York City. She served for three years as assistant to the pastor at Broadway United Church of Christ in New York, and is a member of the National Council of Churches Commission on Faith and Order.

LETTY M. RUSSELL is Assistant Professor of Theology at Yale University Divinity School, New Haven, Connecticut, and Adjunct Professor of New York Theological Seminary. She has also taught at Manhattan College, The Bronx, New York; Union Theological Seminary, New York; Princeton Theological Seminary; and United Theological College, Bangalore, India. She has served as Religious Consultant to the National Board of the YWCA and as Consultant to the U.S. Working Group on the Participation of Women in the World Council of Churches. For ten years, she was pastor of the Presbyterian Church of the Ascension of the East Harlem Protestant Parish. Her most recent book is *Human Liberation in a Feminist Perspective—A Theology* (The Westminster Press, 1974).

VALERIE RUSSELL, as chairperson of the National Council of Churches Task Force on Sexism and the Bible, assisted in the planning and preparation that resulted in writing THE LIBERATING WORD. She is assistant to the president of the United Church of Christ, with responsibility for women's concerns.

NOTES

1. Elizabeth Cady Stanton, *The Woman's Bible* (Seattle: Coalition Task Force on Women and Religion, 1974; orig. published 1895), Part I, p. 5.

2. Sharon Neufer Emswiler and Thomas Neufer Emswiler, *Women and Worship: A Guide to Nonsexist Hymns, Prayers, and Liturgies* (Harper & Row, Publishers, Inc., 1974); *Reformed Liturgy and Music*, Vol. VIII, No. 5 (Fall 1974), revisions of *The Worshipbook*, The Program Agency, The United Presbyterian Church U.S.A.; *Because We Are One People: Songs for Worship* (Ecumenical Women's Centers, 1653 W. School St., Chicago, Ill. 60657, 1974).

3. See Chapter 2. In this book the word "patriarchal" is used to refer to the type of family structure generally found in Biblical times in which the father ruled. "Androcentric" is used to refer to any culture or society that is male-centered in structure, power, and ideas.

4. Rosemary Radford Ruether (ed.), *Religion and Sexism: Images of Woman in the Jewish and Christian Traditions* (Simon & Schuster, Inc., 1974).

5. "Statement from the Consultation on Sexist Language in Theology and Church," Geneva, Feb. 19–22, 1975 (Report to the Executive Committee of the World Council of Churches, April 14–18, 1975, Document No. 8).

6. According to Von Rad, the Biblical view is that we speak of God in human metaphors because we are *theomorphic* (made in God's image) and not because God is *an-*

thropomorphic (made in human image). See Gerhard von Rad, *The Theology of Israel's Historical Traditions,* Vol. I of Old Testament Theology (Harper & Row, Publishers, Inc., 1962), p. 145.

7. Karl Barth, *The Humanity of God* (John Knox Press, 1970), pp. 37–51.

8. The word "feminist" signifies anyone advocating changes that will establish political, economic, social, and ecclesiastical equality of the sexes. It should be distinguished from the biological term "female," and the word "feminine" that refers to a culturally defined set of roles and personal characteristics. See Letty M. Russell, *Human Liberation in a Feminist Perspective—A Theology* (The Westminster Press, 1974), p. 19.

9. Unless otherwise indicated all Bible quotations are from the Revised Standard Version of the Bible, copyright 1946, 1952, 1971, 1973.

10. Sexism is any attitude, action, or institutional structure that systematically subordinates a person or group on grounds of sex. *Nonsexist interpretation is pro-human interpretation* that views male and female as equally made in God's image.

11. The divine name is traditionally written with only its consonants. In Judaism it is never pronounced, but rather the person reading replaces it with "Adonai," "the Lord" (written in large and small capital letters in both the King James and the Revised Standard Versions of the Bible). The practice in Christianity is to name God's name, and when it is pronounced it is vocalized "Yahweh."

12. My own translation.

13. James A. Sanders, *Torah and Canon* (Fortress Press, 1972).

14. Richard E. Palmer, *Hermeneutics* (Northwestern University Press, 1969).

15. Phyllis Trible, "Biblical Theology as Women's Work," *Religion in Life,* Vol. XLIV, No. 1 (Spring 1975). Cf. the research of Cyril Richardson on "Matristics" at Union Theological Seminary, New York.

16. Krister Stendahl, "Biblical Theology, Contemporary," *The Interpreter's Dictionary of the Bible,* ed. by George A. Buttrick (Abingdon Press, 1962), Vol. I, pp. 418–432.

17. Rudolf Bultmann, "Is Exegesis Without Presuppositions

Possible?" *Existence and Faith* (Meridian Books, Inc., 1960), pp. 289–296.

18. Dietrich Bonhoeffer, "What Is Meant by 'Telling the Truth'?" *Ethics*, ed. by Eberhard Bethge (The Macmillan Company, 1955), pp. 363–372.

19. Brevard S. Childs, *Biblical Theology in Crisis* (The Westminster Press, 1970).

20. James Barr, *The Bible in the Modern World* (Harper & Row, Publishers, Inc., 1973); Van A. Harvey, *The Historian and the Believer* (The Macmillan Company, 1966).

21. Robert W. Funk, *Language, Hermeneutic, and Word of God* (Harper & Row, Publishers, Inc., 1966); James M. Robinson and John B. Cobb, *The New Hermeneutic* (Harper & Row, Publishers, Inc., 1964); Palmer, *Hermeneutics;* Hans-Georg Gadamer, *Truth and Method* (The Seabury Press, Inc., 1975).

22. Dorothee Soelle, *Political Theology* (Fortress Press, 1974).

23. José Miranda, *Marx and the Bible* (Orbis Books, 1974).

24. Elizabeth Boyden Howes, *Intersection and Beyond* (Guild for Psychological Studies, Inc., 1971); Walter Wink, *The Bible in Human Transformation* (Fortress Press, 1973); Peter Homans, *Theology After Freud* (The Bobbs-Merrill Co., Inc., 1970).

25. Russell, *Human Liberation in a Feminist Perspective— A Theology;* Soelle, *Political Theology;* Gustavo Gutiérrez, *A Theology of Liberation* (Orbis Books, 1973).

26. Thomas S. Kuhn, *The Structure of Scientific Revolutions*, 2d. ed. rev. (The University of Chicago Press, 1970).

27. John Dominic Crossan (ed.), *SEMEIA 4: Paul Ricoeur on Biblical Hermeneutics* (Society of Biblical Literature, 1975).

28. Cf. R. A. Scroggs, "Paul and the Eschatological Woman," *Journal of the American Academy of Religion (JAAR)*, Vol. XL (1972), p. 5; P. J. Ford, S.J., "Paul the Apostle: Male Chauvinist?" *Biblical Theology Bulletin*, Vol. 5 (1975), pp. 303–311. For a perceptive and supportive account, cf. W. E. Hull, "Woman in Her Place: Biblical Perspectives," *Review and Expositor*, Vol. LXXII (1975), pp. 5–17; cf. pp. 6f.

29. For a more thorough discussion, see my article "Feminist Theology as a Critical Theology of Liberation," *Theological Studies*, Vol. XXXVI, No. 4 (1975), pp. 605–626, 611 ff.,

and the excellent article by J. Lambert, "Un-Fettering the Word: A Call for Coarcial Interpretation of the Bible," *Covenant Quarterly*, May 1974, pp. 3–26.

30. The feminist use of "his story" or "her story" is *not* an etymological explanation, but a wordplay to point out the male bias of all history and historiography. To quote Henry Adams: "The study of history is useful to the historian by teaching him his ignorance of women; and the mass of this ignorance crashes one who is familiar enough with what is called historical sources to realize how few women have ever been known. The woman who is only known through a man is known wrong." (Cf. Mary R. Beard, *Woman as Force in History*, p. 219; The Macmillan Company, 1971.)

31. In writing this section, I found extremely helpful Phyllis Bird's article "Images of Women in the Old Testament," in Ruether (ed.), *Religion and Sexism*, pp. 41–88.

32. Roland de Vaux, *Ancient Israel: Its Life and Institutions* (McGraw-Hill Book Co., Inc., 1961), p. 40.

33. Gerhard von Rad, *Genesis, A Commentary*, rev. ed., The Old Testament Library (The Westminster Press, 1973), pp. 215–222. On p. 218, Von Rad pleads that the text "must not be judged simply by our Western ideas."

34. Hans Wilhelm Hertzberg, *Das Buch der Richter*, Das Alte Testament Deutsch (ATD), 9/19: 3d ed. (Göttingen: Vandenhoeck & Ruprecht, 1965), pp. 254–256, points out that the final redactional remark in Judg. 21:25 attributes the events to the fact that Israel had no king at the time. But Hertzberg argues that the actions against the women were justified because the survival of an Israelite tribe was endangered.

35. See L. Blagg Harter, "The Theme of the Barren Woman in the Patriarchal Narratives," *Concern*, Nov. 1971, pp. 20–24; Dec. 1971, pp. 18–23.

36. Cf. "Images of Women in the Bible," *Women's Caucus Religious Studies Newsletter*, Vol. II, No. 3 (1974), pp. 1–6; J. C. Williams, "Yahweh, Women, and the Trinity," *Theology Today*, Vol. XXXII, No. 3 (Oct. 1975), pp. 234–242, and the unpublished paper of Phyllis Bird, "Masculinity and Monotheism: An Inquiry Into the Limitation of the Feminine in O. T. Representation of the Deity with Attention to Its Sources and

Consequences," delivered at the Southwest Regional Meeting of the Society of Biblical Literature, March 1975.

37. Hans Walter Wolff, *Hosea,* Vol. 4 in the Hermeneia series (Fortress Press, 1974), pp. 48, 14 ff., 24 ff.

38. This tendency is still found in the most recent scholarly Old Testament lexicon, where the Fall is attributed to the fact that the first woman distanced herself from her husband and acted without him (Gen. 3:1–6). Cf. G. Johannes Botterweck and Helmer Ringgren, *Theologisches Wörterbuch zum Alten Testament* (Stuttgart: Verlag W. Kohlhammer, 1971), col. 244 (N. P. Bratsiottis).

39. Cf. Phyllis Bird, "Images of Women in the Old Testament," in Ruether (ed.), *Religion and Sexism,"* pp. 87n, 88, who contests the argument that *'ādām* is understood as an androgynous being. Cf. Phyllis Trible, "Depatriarchalization in Biblical Interpretation," *JAAR,* Vol. XLI (1973), pp. 30–49, 35.

40. Claus Westermann, *Genesis,* Biblischer Kommentar: Altes Testament (Neukirchen: Vluyn, 1970), pp. 245 ff.

41. Herbert Lockyer, *The Women of the Bible* (Zondervan Publishing House, 1967), pp. 113 f.

42. Michael Cardinal von Faulhaber, *Women of the Bible,* ed. by Brendan Keogh (The Newman Press, 1955), pp. 50f.

43. Martin Noth, *Das vierte Buch Mose: Numeri,* ATD 7 (Göttingen: Vandenhoeck & Ruprecht, 1966), pp. 84 f.

44. For a more detailed argumentation, cf. my article "The Role of Women in the Early Christian Movement," *Concilium,* Vol. VII (1976).

45. Leonard Swidler, "Is Sexism a Sign of Decadence in Religion?" in Judith Plaskow and Joan A. Romero (eds.), *Women and Religion,* rev. ed. (Scholars Press, 1974), pp. 170 f.

46. Cf. my book, *Der vergessene Partner, Grundlagen, Tatsachen und Möglichkeiten der Mitarbeit der Frau in der Kirche* (Düsseldorf: Patmos Verlag, 1964), pp. 57–59, 125–127.

47. In my sermon "Mary Magdalene, Apostle to the Apostles," *UTS Journal,* April 1975, pp. 22 f., I have pointed out that, according to the Pauline and Lucan criteria of apostleship, Mary Magdalene and the other women were apostles, since they accompanied Jesus and had seen the resurrected Lord. R. E. Brown accepts this suggestion but then plays down

this insight: "The priority given to Peter in Paul and in Luke is a priority among those who became *official* [italics mine] witnesses to the Resurrection. The secondary place given to the tradition of an appearance to a woman or women probably reflects the fact that women did not serve at first as official preachers of the Church—a fact that would make the creation of an appearance to a woman unlikely." (Cf. Brown's article "Roles of Women in the Fourth Gospel," *Theological Studies,* Vol. XXXVI, No. 4 (1975), pp. 688–699, 692n12). I do not understand what the qualification "official" means in a situation where church offices were in the stage of development and when we know that women had leading roles as prophets, apostles, and missionaries in the early Christian communities. It is problematic to project later church institutional forms back into the early church.

48. Scroggs, "Paul and the Eschatological Woman," pp. 5–17; W. A. Meeks, "The Image of the Androgyne," *History of Religion,* Vol. XIII (1974), pp. 165–208; W. Munro, "Patriarchy and Charismatic Community," in Plaskow and Romero (eds.), *Women and Religion,* pp. 189–198; W. O. Walker, "I Corinthians 11:2–16 and Paul's View Regarding Woman," *Journal of Biblical Literature (JBL),* Vol. XCIV (1975), pp. 94–110.

49. J. E. Crouch, *The Origin and Intention of the Colossian Haustafel* (Göttingen: Vandenhoeck & Ruprecht, 1972). John Howard Yoder, *The Politics of Jesus* (Wm. B. Eerdmans Publishing Company, 1972), pp. 163–192, however, argues that the concept of subordination is a specific Christian concept. See his argument against Krister Stendahl's position (*The Bible and the Role of Women: A Case Study in Hermeneutics;* Fortress Press, 1966): "What if, for instance, the sweeping, doctrinaire egalitarianism of our culture, which makes the concept of the 'place of woman' seem laughable or boorish and makes that of 'subordination' seem insulting, should turn out really (in the 'intent of God' or in long-run social experience) to be demonic, uncharitable, destructive of personality, disrespectful of creation, and unworkable?" (p. 177n22).

50. For the wider context, see my article "Apocalyptic and Gnosis in the Book of Revelation and Paul," *JBL,* Vol. XCII (1973), pp. 565–581.

51. Judith Plaskow, "The Coming of Lilith," in Ruether (ed.), *Religion and Sexism,* pp. 341–343.

52. Cf. Katherine D. Sackenfeld, "The Bible and Women: Bane or Blessing?" *Theology Today,* Vol. XXXII, No. 3 (Oct. 1975), pp. 222–233; cf. p. 228. Sackenfeld speaks about the danger of searching for "timeless truth" that "seems to transcend the normally expected cultural biases of the author" because new biases about what is "timeless" are often introduced. Although revelation occurs within the human sphere and it is not possible to make absolute identification of such "truths," it is possible to look for points at which the liberating Word of God seems to have broken through cultural patterns on behalf of the oppressed.

53. Bird, "Images of Women in the Old Testament," in Ruether (ed.), *Religion and Sexism,* p. 41.

54. I am indebted to Phyllis Trible, "Depatriarchalization in Biblical Interpretation," p. 34, for calling my attention to this passage.

55. Hans Walter Wolff, "The Elohist Fragments in the Pentateuch," *Interpretation,* Vol. XXVI (1972), p. 165.

56. Trible, "Depatriarchalization in Biblical Interpretation," p. 34.

57. In Hebrew, "the prophetess."

58. In the Hebrew and in Jewish translations, the verses are Joel 3:1–2.

59. There are problems both with the dating of The Book of Joel and with whether or not all the writings in the book derive from one author, but they do not materially affect the discussion here.

60. See Samuel Terrien, "Toward a Biblical Theology of Womanhood," *Religion in Life,* Vol. XLI (Autumn 1973), p. 330.

61. The translations from Mark 7:24–30 are my own.

62. Some ancient texts add "your sisters."

63. Mark 3:31–35. My own translation.

64. Joachim Jeremias, *Jerusalem in the Time of Jesus.* (Fortress Press, 1969), p. 375.

65. Quoted in Jeremias, *ibid.,* p. 373.

66. Bird, "Images of Women in the Old Testament," in Ruether (ed.), *Religion and Sexism,* pp. 55, 57.

67. Constance F. Parvey, "The Theology and Leadership of Women in the New Testament," in Ruether (ed.), *Religion and Sexism,* p. 134.

68. There is no pronoun, masculine or feminine, in the Greek text.

69. For the following discussion, I am much indebted to Krister Stendahl, *The Bible and the Role of Women: A Case Study in Hermeneutics,* pp. 28–37.

70. Rachel Conrad Wahlberg, *Jesus According to a Woman* (Paulist/Newman Press, 1975).

71. Letha Scanzoni and Nancy Hardesty, *All We're Meant to Be: A Biblical Approach to Women's Liberation* (Word Books, 1974), pp. 54–59.

72. Sakae Kubo and Walter Specht, *So Many Versions? Twentieth Century English Versions of the Bible* (Zondervan Publishing House, 1975), pp. 13–19. George Tavard points out that linguistic science does not recognize a direct correlation between social structures and those of language, but it is obvious that at various levels and in various ways changes in social consciousness and culture have an influence on language and symbol. "Sexist Language in Theology," *Theological Studies,* Vol. XXXVI, No. 4 (1975), p. 704.

73. Letty M. Russell, *Christian Education in Mission* (The Westminster Press, 1967), pp. 77–80.

74. Stendahl, *The Bible and the Role of Women,* p. 32; Alice Hageman (ed.), *Sexist Religion and Women in the Church: No More Silence!* (Association Press, 1974), pp. 119–120.

75. Scanzoni and Hardesty, *All We're Meant to Be,* Ch. 5, "Woman's Best Friend: Jesus," pp. 54–59; Wahlberg, *Jesus According to a Woman.*

76. For example, see *Report from the Task Force on Women in Church and Society,* which contains recommendations that were adopted by the Tenth General Synod of the United Church of Christ, June 1974.

77. For example, see *Reformed Liturgy and Music,* Vol. VIII, No. 5, and "Statement from the Consultation on Sexist Language in Theology and Church," Geneva, Feb. 19–22, 1975.

78. See "Additional Resources," Sec. III; and Alma Graham, "The Language of Unequal Opportunity," *A.D.,* Feb. 1975,

pp. 32–35. Linguistically speaking, gender does not necessarily suggest the sex of a word, but in English, where there are only three genders (masculine, feminine, and neuter), gender and sex are closely linked in popular thought. Therefore the use of male pronouns helps to reinforce the cycle of sexist assumptions. Tavard states that we should not bother with linguistic gender questions, but should demand "a reform in depth of our symbolisms" ("Sexist Language in Theology," p. 714). I think that for most people these symbolisms are linked to language usage, if not directly to gender, and should be addressed in the struggle to change attitudes and actions.

79. See "Additional Resources," Sec. I, and Sakenfeld, "The Bible and Women: Bane or Blessing?" p. 231; Paul D. Hanson, "Masculine Metaphors for God and Sex Discrimination in the Old Testament," *The Ecumenical Review,* Vol. XXVII, No. 4 (Oct. 1975), pp. 320–322.

80. See "Additional Resources," Sec. III, and *The Ecumenical Review,* Vol. XXVII, No. 4 (Oct. 1975), pp. 386–393.

81. H. Richard Niebuhr, *The Responsible Self* (Harper & Row, Publishers, Inc., 1963), p. 103.

82. Paul Tillich, *Dynamics of Faith* (Harper & Row, Publishers, Inc., 1957), pp. 42–43.

83. Report of the Advisory Council on Discipleship and Worship on the Language About God, "Opening the Door" (The Program Agency, The United Presbyterian Church U.S.A., 1975), p. 13.

84. Bird, "Masculinity and Monotheism: An Inquiry Into the Limitation of the Feminine in O.T. Representations of the Deity with Attention to Its Sources and Consequences."

85. Russell, *Human Liberation in a Feminist Perspective— A Theology* pp. 96–103; Tavard, "Sexist Language in Theology," p. 721.

86. Russell, *Human Liberation in a Feminist Perspective— A Theology,* pp. 135–140.

87. Catherine Gunsalus Gonzales, "Reflections on Language of Deity and Worship." Unpublished address delivered at the Women's Interseminary Conference, Pittsburgh, March 1975.

88. Hanson, "Masculine Metaphors for God and Sex Discrimination in the Old Testament," p. 317.

89. Russell, *Human Liberation in a Feminist Perspective—A Theology,* pp. 101–102; Tavard, "Sexist Language in Theology," pp. 720–723.

90. Trible, "Biblical Theology as Women's Work," p. 7.

91. *Reformed Liturgy and Music,* Vol. VIII, No. 5, p. 24.

92. Sakenfeld, "The Bible and Women: Bane or Blessing?" p. 225.

ADDITIONAL RESOURCES

I. *Background Books*

Daly, Mary. *The Church and the Second Sex.* Harper & Row, Publishers, Inc., 1968.

Dewey, Joanna, *Disciples of the Way: Mark on Discipleship.* Women's Division, Board of Global Ministries, The United Methodist Church, 1976.

Emswiler, Sharon Neufer, and Emswiler, Thomas Neufer. *Women and Worship: A Guide to Nonsexist Hymns, Prayers, and Liturgies.* Harper & Row, Publishers, Inc., 1974.

Faxon, Alicia Craig. *Women and Jesus.* United Church Press, 1973.

Hewitt, Emily C., and Hiatt, Susan R. *Women Priests: Yes or No?* The Seabury Press, Inc., 1973.

Jewett, Paul K. *Man as Male and Female.* Wm. B. Eerdmans Publishing Company, 1975.

Kress, Robert. *Wither Womankind? The Humanity of Women.* Abbey Press, 1975.

Ruether, Rosemary Radford. *New Women and New Earth: Sexist Ideologies and Human Liberation.* The Seabury Press, Inc., 1975; (ed.) *Religion and Sexism: Images of Woman in the Jewish and Christian Traditions.* Simon & Schuster, Inc., 1974.

Russell, Letty M. *Human Liberation in a Feminist Perspective —A Theology.* The Westminster Press, 1974.

Scanzoni, Letha, and Hardesty, Nancy. *All We're Meant to Be:*

A Biblical Approach to Women's Liberation. Word Books,
1974.

Stanton, Elizabeth Cady. *The Woman's Bible.* (2 parts in 1).
Republished, Seattle: Coalition Task Force on Women and
Religion, 1974.

Tavard, George H. *Woman in Christian Tradition.* University
of Notre Dame Press, 1973.

Wahlberg, Rachel Conrad. *Jesus According to a Woman.* Paul-
ist/Newman Press, 1975.

II. *Articles*

See the notes to each chapter for articles and references to
specific materials on each topic.

III. *Guides to Nonsexist Language*

*Guidelines for Equal Treatment of the Sexes in McGraw-Hill
Book Company Publications,* distributed by McGraw-Hill
Book Company, 1221 Avenue of the Americas, New York,
N.Y. 10020.

Guidelines for Screening Bias for Writers and Editors, distributed by the Office of Communications, Lutheran
Church in America, 231 Madison Ave. New York, N.Y.
10012.

"Linguistic Sexism," editorial by Leonard Swidler in *Journal
of Ecumenical Studies,* Vol. II, No. 2 (Spring 1974). Also
available from the Task Force on Women, United Church
of Christ, 297 Park Ave. S., New York, N.Y. 10010.

Reformed Liturgy and Music, Vol. VIII, No. 5 (Fall 1974),
revisions of *The Worshipbook,* The Program Agency, The
United Presbyterian Church U.S.A., 475 Riverside Drive,
New York, N.Y. 10027.

Report of the Advisory Council on Discipleship and Worship
on the Language About God, "Opening the Door," The
Program Agency, The United Presbyterian Church U.S.A.
475 Riverside Drive, New York, N.Y. 10027.

IV. *Other Resources*

Because We Are One People: Songs for Worship, Ecumenical Women's Centers, 1653 W. School St., Chicago, Ill. 60657.

Included Out, 2-minute film on language in worship, by Sharon Neufer Emswiler, distributed by Mass Media Industries, 2116 N. Charles St., Baltimore, Md. 21218.

Russell, Letty M. "The Freedom of God," Twelve Bible studies, *Enquiry,* Vol. 8, No. 1 (Sept.–Nov. 1975), pp. 27–48. The Geneva Press, 1132 Witherspoon Bldg., Philadelphia, Pa. 19107.

Sing a Womansong, Ecumenical Women's Centers, 1653 W. School St., Chicago, Ill. 60657.